FACETS

Selected Titles in the Facets Series

Visionary Women: Three Medieval Mystics
Rosemary Radford Ruether

On Christian Liberty
Martin Luther

Who Is Christ for Us?
Dietrich Bonhoeffer

The Call to Discipleship
Karl Barth

Christian Faith and Religious Diversity
Edited by John B. Cobb Jr.

The Measure of a Man
Martin Luther King Jr.

The Wit of Martin Luther

Eric W. Gritsch

Fortress Press
Minneapolis

THE WIT OF MARTIN LUTHER

Cover image: Portrait of the young Martin Luther by Lucas Cranach the Elder. Germanisches Nationalmuseum, Nuremberg, Germany.
Photo: © Scala/Art Resource, NY

Library of Congress Cataloging-in-Publication Data
ISBN-13: 978-0-8006-3803-0

Manufactured in the U.S.A.

Contents

Let us laugh at raging Satan and the world
(yes, even at sin and our conscience in us).
—Martin Luther, LW 12:25

If you are going to tell people the truth,
you'd better make them laugh.
Otherwise, they'll kill you.
—George Bernard Shaw

Humor is, in fact, the prelude to faith;
and laughter is the beginning of prayer.
—Reinhold Niebuhr, *Humor and Faith*, 111.

Preface

What's so funny about Luther? Luther's humor is a stepchild, as it were, in Luther research. Since its inception in 1956, the International Congress for Luther Research has not dealt with the role of humor in the life and work of the Wittenberg reformer. No major study has been published on this subject.

Nathan Söderblom (1866–1931) once offered a sketch of Luther's humor, combined with melancholy.[1] The Swedish archbishop and historian of religion described Luther's humor as "above all the resting-point and safety-valve of a tremendously tense soul" that rejected any human fashioning of "the holy." While humor created relief from anxiety, melancholy helped Luther

> to dig deep into a depth where he could recognize his own nothingness and collect the light to see the helping grace; so he was strengthened to console others and become a true 'doctor of consolation' (*doctor consolator*). In this sense, humor and melancholy became the components of a religious frame centered in the evangelical trust in God which ended what had slumbered before in every human breast—the fear of pride (*hybris*) and its punishment. That is why humor and melancholy are peculiar, fortifying additions to the enduring, common needs of the heart.

Söderblom shows how the dialectic of humor and melancholy strengthened Luther's faith and enabled him to survive such crises as the condemnation at Worms (1521), the peasants' rebellion, and the encounter with Erasmus of Rotterdam (1525). Söderblom offers a psycho-historical review of Luther's religious disposition, linking it to mysticism as a generic part of the "history of religion" (*Religionsgeschichte*).[2]

The Swiss church historian Fritz Blanke highlighted Luther's humor in pastoral care, offering samples from Luther's work as counselor and pastor in his Wittenberg congregation.[3] I have published some essays on Luther's humor.[4] An old friend, the Rev. Dr. Joseph A. Burgess, prodded me to write this little book. He also supplied me with literature dealing with the subject of humor more generally.

It is puzzling why the almost unfathomable literature on Luther lists nothing else on his humor, and why scholars have not dealt with its role in the life and work of the great reformer. After all, he has been studied in detail, analyzed psychologically, and acknowledged as a legitimate "father of the church," even within Roman Catholicism. It is time to take his humor seriously.

Throughout this little book, I quote Luther extensively because I want the reader to get a sense and taste of his extraordinary use of humor in the context of his unusual life and thought. Moreover, his humor, like a good joke, needs to be experienced "in the nude" (as he might say!). It has to speak for itself, especially in the manner in which Luther was able to turn a humorous phrase for God.

The first chapter shows *how* humor became an integral part of his work as a reformer. The second chapter *illustrates* his humor in telling examples of his work as an interpreter of the Bible, in his pastoral care, and in his encounter with mortality. The third chapter depicts *why* his anticipation of the Last Day made Luther not only serene but also free. Dealing with this question made me realize that Luther's humor in its eschatological setting is a mark of freedom in his life and work. He has been acknowledged as a "theologian of the cross." But his kind of humor also discloses a "theology of freedom," which should become the most attractive component of his enduring legacy.

Some readers of Luther see much humor in his graphic description of sexuality and in his derogatory sayings about women, based on the medieval view that they are inferior to men. But such a reading is done with *Schadenfreude*—enjoying the troubles of others, in this case, the self-incriminating wit of a Luther who is no longer "respectable."[5] I have included some of this material in the "Witticisms" of the appendix. But Luther's chauvinism is overshadowed by his love and respect for Katie, whose charm, intelligence, and business sense enhanced—indeed fueled—the life and work of the Wittenberg reformer. Katie was the "rib" (Gen. 2:22) that became his funny-bone when she joined him in marriage almost five centuries ago (1525).

Quotations and footnotes use texts from the German-Latin Weimar Edition and their translation in the American Edition of *Luther's Works*. Unless noted otherwise, all other translations are mine. The bibliography consists only of pertinent sources. Updated literature on Luther is available in the annual edition of the *Lutherjahrbuch*.

I chose "wit" as the single word to describe Luther's use of humor. It describes a quick mind that can tell a "joke" (*Witz* in German), knows how to have fun through "jesting" (*scherzen* in German), and is a "wag" (*Schalk* in German). Luther presented himself as a "court jester" (*Hofnarr* in German, "a fool at court") to German politicians, and he was an amusing wit (*Spassvogel* in German, "a funny bird") at the dinner table. His wit relaxed anxious minds and annoyed angry foes. May it continue to do so today.

Introduction

Humor can be thought of as "the mental faculty of discovering, expressing, or appreciating the ludicrous or absurdly incongruous."[1] In other words, some minds are able to make room for something that is inconsistent, irrational, and has no satisfactory meaning. They know what is rational; but they also know the limits of their thinking. So they smile—maybe even laugh—about experiencing an intellectual dead end.

Humor is thus anchored in a self-knowledge that indicates one's limitations. Such insight is a mark of human maturity and freedom, expressed in the ability to joke about oneself. Conversely, lack of humor means the *loss* of the freedom to face one's own limitations. People without a sense of humor are like dried fruit, perhaps attractive at the time of harvest, but later repugnant and boring. Truly mature people have a sense of humor that is open for many attitudes, ranging from the sublime to the ridiculous. They encounter life's reality in its true power. That is why "humor does not tolerate a presumed superiority and leads human self-knowledge again back from its imaged height to the right track."[2] Or, to put it less academically, "A sense of humor is a measurement of the extent to which we realize

1

that we are trapped in a world almost totally devoid of reason. Laughter is how we express the anxiety we feel at this knowledge."[3]

Having humor presupposes some education. That is why preschool children ask funny questions without a sense of humor. They just demand an answer to everything that comes to their minds: Why don't horses fly like birds? Do fleas cough? Do noodles grow on trees? They have not learned yet how to deal with the absurd and therefore have little room for humor. Linguists observe that the word "humor" stems from the Latin *umor* meaning "moisture," or "fluid." The same word used in ancient Rome for milk and wine described body fluids in the Middle Ages. The English word "humour" (from the French *humeur*) appeared for the first time in 1682 to describe comedies.[4] Serious investigations of humor seem to yield little to laugh about. So *lector caveat*—reader, beware not to get too serious about "theoretical" analyses of humor!

Luther is not listed among the great humorists. Perhaps the turbulent context of his life and work hide his relaxation as a theologian who had gained the self-critical maturity to respect the absurd and smile about it. His time was full of fear of the wrath of God; of plagues, and of social unrest which created chaos; and it seemed as if Satan had his way with the church—Luther's favorite way of describing evil, or something that goes wrong. He himself experienced condemnation by church and state; he endured debilitating spiritual, mental, and physical problems; but he lived through all the perils of his life and work with an almost uncanny sense of freedom laced with humor.

Luther said that his severe spiritual struggle (*Anfechtung* in German, *tentatio* in Latin, "temptation") made him a theologian focused on Christ as the mediator of salvation from sin, evil, and death.[5] This focus made him a "theologian of the cross" as well as a "theologian of freedom": he was called to serve others, even if suffering was involved, and he viewed his life already as a life with God beyond death. The foundation of his cruciform and liberating theology is found in the final part of his classic treatise, *The Freedom of the Christian* (1520):

> A Christian lives not to himself, but in Christ and his neighbor. Otherwise he is not a Christian. He lives in Christ through faith, in his neighbor through love. By faith he is caught up beyond himself into God. By love he descends beneath himself into his neighbor. Yet he always remains in God and in his love, as Christ says in John 1[:51], "Truly, truly, I say to you, *you will see heaven opened* and the angels of God ascending and descending upon the Son of Man."[6]

Free *from* oneself? Free *for* others? Caught up into God? Descending into the neighbor?

Yet always remaining in God? This is a most peculiar, indeed irrational, description of how faith and love are to work together!

This description of the Christian life speaks not only of a relationship with Christ and the neighbor, but also assumes the second coming of Christ. Thus Luther presupposes the biblical Christian view of life as the interim, the meantime between the resurrection of Jesus and his return at the end of time, on the Last Day. Christians are people on "the Way" (Acts 24:14) to a future "where righteousness is at home" (2 Peter 3:1); they are "strangers and foreigners on earth" (Heb. 11:13) on the way to the eternal "city of God" (Heb. 11:16).

Luther saw his whole life shaped by this view of life as interim, analogous to the interim between his own birth and death—a mere sixty-two years (November 10, 1483, to February 18, 1546). He expected the end of the world in his own lifetime; he even constructed his own chronology, following the traditional medieval scheme of viewing world history as a succession of seven millennia, analogous to the ages of Adam, Noah, Abraham, David, Christ, the pope (as the embodiment of the antichrist), and the final reign of Christ.[7] But he never published or proclaimed this chronological construction and never disclosed any anxiety about it, as did millenarians before and after him.

According to Luther, the struggle between his reform movement and the papal church was the meanest part of the mean meantime between the first and second advent of Christ. But he was confident that Christ would triumph over the devil, and so he remained cheerful in his eschatological orientation. This point of view was his consolation in a life that seemed hopeless to others, and it was also a restraint for his theology when it tended to become too speculative. Thus he summarized his difficult and busy life in words that exhibited a gallows humor with a scatological twist. "I'm like a ripe stool," he said to his wife Katie shortly before his death, "and the world's like a gigantic anus, and we're about to let go of each other."[8] His rejection of theological speculation is clothed in satire. When asked where God was before the creation of the world, Luther replied (quoting his favorite church father, St. Augustine), "God was making hell for those who are inquisitive."[9]

Humor was for Luther the guard to prevent him from crossing the frontier to speculation about God and human life beyond its earthly existence—the enduring temptation of theologians and philosophers to try to discover the hidden God. Luther is a theologian who tried to become liberated from this temptation by clinging to the revealed God, "the father of Jesus Christ." In this sense, his theology is marked by freedom—"the freedom of the glory of the children of God" (Rom. 8:21). This freedom generates true joy, firmly anchored in the faith that salvation from evil, sin, and death

comes through Christ. But joyous laughing and
sad crying always struggle with each other:

> When we should cry, because of our sin,
> we laugh. When we should laugh, because
> of our rejoicing in Christ who died for us
> so that we have eternal life, we cry. For we
> do not value such joy higher than other
> worldly joys which we cherish. But when sin
> and divine wrath strike our heart we neither
> want nor are able to be consoled."[10]

1

The Power of Serenity

Saved from Being Deadly Serious

Luther was a very serious, zealous student, monk, priest, and professor of biblical studies. Powerful superstitions in his time—like belief in demons, witches, and the power of the devil—provided a challenging context to pursue an ambitious career in the church, the institution of salvation from the perils of earthly life. Luther learned early in life that the devil can only be faced, chased, and defeated by the intervention of God in Christ. Above all, Luther was taught that one should not be alone when in spiritual distress: "Those who are troubled with melancholy...ought to be very careful not to be alone, for God created the fellowship of the church and commanded brotherliness." He also was taught as a monk that noisy cursing and especially scatological language are the first lines of defense against the devil, followed by prayer. Since the devil likes to argue and to confuse ("diabolical" comes from the Greek verb *diaballein*—"to set things apart by throwing them"), one must resist him with power, indeed with physical expressions of disgusting relief. "I resist the devil," Luther is quoted as saying, "and often it is with a fart that I chase him away."[1]

School was no fun. At age ten Martin attended a class where the teacher appointed one of the students to catch the other students in violations of discipline, such as speaking German (only Latin was allowed). At the end of the week violators were punished. The worst offender had to wear a wooden donkey around his neck; he was allowed to hang it on a fellow student who had switched into German. Luther spent his early teens in a parochial school in the town of Eisenach where life was less severe. Students often sang with adults and worked as "crumb collectors" (*Partekenhengst*) in the street, begging for food.

Luther had obeyed his father and studied law, the best secular career for a commoner. But he was too restless about his spiritual future, being constantly surrounded by the church's threat of divine wrath for those who do not strive for spiritual perfection. That is why Luther vowed to become a monk. A frightening thunderstorm was the final push to withdraw from the world. The "terrors from heaven" and the "agony of sudden death" did it, Luther told his father.[2] The threat of heavenly terror dominated the sermons of priests and monks who often sold "indulgences" in certificates of satisfaction substituting for the good works one is unable or unwilling to do. According to the catechetical instruction of Luther's time, believers had to appease the wrath of God through merits. Accumulating them was no mean task, and people streamed to the confessionals to indicate their penance for sins and to receive absolution from them by sacrificing time and money. But striving for spiritual satisfaction was a bottomless pit; confessed sins simply begat more. This was the point at which Luther's deadly serious attention to penance produced a suicidal anxiety. He felt like a soldier in a panic-stricken army, frightened by the sound of a falling leaf (Lev. 26:36). When spiritual counselors and "father confessors" admonished Luther to try harder, to pull himself up by his bootstraps, as it were, Luther despaired because there were no more straps on which to pull. Finding these resources within himself was impossible, since he felt that his self was itself threatened with annihilation. Help, any sense of sanity, had to come from the outside.

This need for outside intervention to shore up sanity is what gave rise to Luther's use of humor. As modern reflections on humor observe, humor is found in another human being, be it a friend or a therapist. Since it is from others, humor tells us that life has meaning only in communion with others and that egotistic self-reliance is ridiculous. Real living begins with freedom from the tyranny of the self, and just as a patriotic comedian can make fun of his own country, one can love oneself while joking about it.

Luther finally found peace of mind in a spiritual breakthrough from belief in an angry God to faith in a gracious God who loves the ungodly without their merit—one is right with God, "justified," by complete trust in the merits of someone else, Jesus Christ (Rom. 3:21-26; 4:5). In him one sees a future free from the terrorist network of evil, sin, and death. That is how one acquires a true sense of freedom as a foretaste of a new life that is to come.

Johann von Staupitz, the vicar-general of Luther's order, was instrumental in dragging Luther out of the mire of his spiritual anxiety, an anxiety caused by the fear of punishment by an angry God. Staupitz was impressed with Luther's intellectual abilities but was puzzled by the intensity of Luther's spiritual distress. The young monk and priest sounded like a seminarian or divinity school student doing fine academic work but who always failed his psychology tests, indicating an abnormal personal spirituality. When Luther constantly raised the question, "Why is God so unjust in treating people?" Staupitz answered, "God strikes us for our own good, in order that He might free us who otherwise would be crushed."[3]

Doing penance, he told Luther, is not intended to appease an angry God through bitter-faced good works, but to engage in a spiritual exercise concentrating on God's love for sinners through the cross of Christ. Finally, when Luther still continued to gush forth his stream of confessions and complaints,

Staupitz, like a wise Marine officer, gave Luther a direct order: "You must become a doctor and a preacher. This way you will be kept busy." Luther objected, "You will bring me to my death! I will never endure it for three months." But Staupitz had his way: "Don't you know that our Lord God has many matters to attend to? For these he needs wise and clever people to advise him. If you should die, you will be received into his council in heaven because he too has need of some doctors."[4] Luther had the choice of disobeying a direct order and leaving the monastery—only to be left alone in his despair—or to study for the doctor's degree in biblical studies. Staupitz was the Bible professor at Wittenberg University and, given his impending retirement, was looking for a successor. Young Friar Martin seemed just right for the job.

Luther confessed later that his doctorate saved his life and provided the only legitimate foundation for his call to reform the church: "I would not exchange my doctor's degree for all the world's gold.... I entered into this work publicly and by virtue of my office as teacher and preacher."[5]

The academic vocation of teaching and researching Scripture liberated Luther from the bondage of spiritual despair and forced him to seek help outside himself, in the Bible and in his exposure to others. He learned from the Bible that "penance" (*poenitentia* in Latin, *metanoia* in Greek, "change of mind") did not mean to accuse oneself of not doing enough to appease God's wrath but rather meant a joyful turning to Christ by faith alone. He told Staupitz:

> I began to compare your statements with the passages of Scripture which speak of *poenitentia*. And behold—what a most pleasant scene! Biblical words came leaping toward me from all sides, clearly smiling and nodding assent to your statement. They so supported your opinion that while formerly almost no word in the whole Scripture was more bitter to me than *poenitentia* (although I zealously made a pretense before God and tried to express a feigned and constrained love for him), now no word sounds sweeter or more pleasant to me than *poenitentia*. The commandments of God become sweet when they are read not only in books but also in the wounds of the sweetest Savior.[6]

Teaching young students in a course on Psalms also helped Luther to get away from himself and gain a more lighthearted mood. He threw himself into work. "I hardly have any uninterrupted time to say the Hourly Prayers and celebrate [mass]," he wrote to a close friend. "Besides all this there are my struggles of the flesh, the world and the devil. *See what a lazy man I am*!"[7]

Luther interpreters, especially polemicists, have had some satirical fun with Luther's description of a location where he found solace from his distress: In the "tower room" (*Turmstube*) of the Wittenberg monastery and in its lavatory (*cloaca* in Latin), the only "heated room" (*hypocaustum*), called "the secret room of the monks." A "tower experience" on the toilet? Luther himself may have enjoyed the discreet smiles of his dinner guests when he said, "The Holy Spirit unveiled the Scriptures for me in this tower at the lavatory." [8]

Luther was probably twenty-four years old when he experienced the radical change from a long-lasting depression to a liberating experience of "justification by faith alone." The spiritual depression was severe:

> Though I lived as a monk without reproach, I felt that I was a sinner before God with an extremely disturbed conscience. I could not believe that he was placated by my satisfaction. I did not love, yes, I hated the righteous God who punishes sinners, and secretly, if not blasphemously, certainly murmuring greatly, I was angry with God, and said, "As if, indeed, it is not enough that miserable sinners, eternally lost through original sin, are crushed by every kind of calamity by the law of the decalogue, without having God add pain to pain by the gospel and also by the gospel threatening us with his righteousness and wrath!" Thus I raged with a fierce and troubled conscience.[9]

Luther raced through the Bible to discover a way out from his spiritual blind alley. "Meditating day and night," he finally found peace in the words, "The one who is righteous will live by faith" (Rom. 1:17):

> Here I felt that *I was altogether born again*
> and had entered paradise itself through open
> gates. There a totally other face of the entire
> Scripture showed itself to me. Thereupon I
> ran through the Scriptures from memory. I
> also found in other terms an analogy, as the
> work of God, that is, what God does in us,
> the power of God, with which he makes us
> strong, the wisdom of God, with which he
> makes us wise, the strength of God, the salva-
> tion of God, the glory of God. And I extolled
> my sweetest word with a love as great as the
> hatred with which I had before hated the
> word "righteousness of God."[10]

The "bad news" of the church, admonishing
believers to do hopeless good works, was
replaced by the "good news," the gospel,
promising salvation from sin through
divine grace. Luther's whole being was
permeated by the certainty that God was no
longer against him but for him through the
mediation of the crucified and resurrected
Christ. This certainty made the ecclesiastical
network of penance look like a cruel, indeed
deadly, practical joke. Luther felt that he had
no choice but to attack the church's abuse
of frightened souls and call for a thorough
reform of church and of society from top to
bottom, "in head and in members"—a slogan
known since the thirteenth century. At stake
was a radical reconsideration of creed and
deed, reflecting the certainty that salvation is
an external gift of sheer divine grace rather
than the result of an internal struggle against

guilt through meritorious good works. As Luther put it,

> And this is the reason why our theology is certain: *it snatches us away from ourselves and places us outside ourselves*, so that we do not depend on our own strength, conscience, experience, person, or works *but depend on that which is outside ourselves*, that is, on the promise and truth of God, which cannot deceive.[11]

Jester at the Court of Public Opinion

Luther's spiritual rebirth estranged him from his own church and convinced him that crude ecclesiastical abuses, such as the sale of indulgences, must be removed and the church must be reformed. He would soon discover that the indulgences revealed a spiritual bankruptcy on the part of the ecclesiastical hierarchy and a theological betrayal of the gospel, the "good news" that salvation from sin is a matter of trust in God through Christ rather than a business transaction. Thus the lines were drawn for the priest-professor from Wittenberg: either remain silent and forgo any defense of the gospel as a theologian of the church, or call for the reform of the church that had gone astray, indeed betrayed the gospel for the sake of its own institutional glory.

How should Luther go about reform? Should he be a raging revivalist preaching hell and damnation? An unworldly monk praying for renewal but remaining on the sidelines? An academic critic taking potshots at the most obvious targets?

Luther chose to make his first appearance as a reformer in the guise of a court jester. He raised humorous, satirical questions in his now-famous *Ninety-Five Theses* (1517), which asked for a public disputation on the abuse of selling indulgences with the fraudulent advertising slogan, "As soon as the coin in the coffer rings, a soul from purgatory springs." Thesis Twenty-Nine, for instance, asks, "Who knows whether all souls in purgatory wish to be redeemed, since we have exceptions in St. Severinus and St. Paschal, as related in a legend."[12]

Court jesters had since antiquity been part of an honored political tradition. They entertained powerful rulers with a ready wit, displayed in jokes and commentaries on current events; they were entertainers and wore the dress of fools who often appeared in plays, usually comedies. Dressed in clownish clothes, always wearing an ornate cap with bells, they sometimes rode a donkey into a solemn assembly, mocking etiquette and giving political advice. Court jesters made people laugh about anything, no matter how serious and holy. They, like their noble sponsors, had their own majesty of laughter, as it were, reminding everyone that there is no human perfection; life can always become a joke. They enjoyed extraordinary immunity and rarely suffered persecution; they were the darlings of courtly life, often used as the mouthpiece of a nobleman who wanted to communicate unpopular opinions under the cover of laughter.[13]

Luther did his first "serious" jesting in a literary exchange with one of his first opponents, the Franciscan monk and theologian Augustine Alveld from Leipzig. Employing the tactics of crude polemics among intellectuals during their literary feuds, Alveld had called Luther a "wolf among sheep," a "heretic," and a "madman." Luther retorted that the Leipzig monk was impolite, ignorant, and vain. But the Wittenberg professor, though furious, tamed his response with humor:

This blasphemer values and treats the holy words of God no better than if they had been invented by some fool or jester to use as stories during Shrovetide. Therefore, since my Lord Christ and his holy word, which he dearly purchased with his precious blood, are considered a mockery and foolish talk, *I have to drop my own seriousness and see whether I, too, have learned to play the fool and to mock.* You, my Lord Jesus Christ, know how my heart feels about these arch-blasphemers—that is what I am relying on. Let justice be done in your name, Amen.

I notice that these poor people seek no more than to make a name for themselves at my expense. They cling to me like dirt to a wheel. They would rather have a disgraceful uproar than stay at home. The evil spirit uses

the schemes of such people only to prevent
me from doing better things. But I welcome
this as *an opportunity to teach laymen
something about Christendom* and to combat
these alluring masters.[14]

Here Luther echoes Paul who told his difficult,
often stubborn congregation in Corinth that
sometimes one has to be a fool for the sake
of Christ (1 Cor. 4:10). Such a fool may be
humble and endure persecution, or he may
become a satirist to fend off hostile people.
Luther did that in his attack of Alveld. After
a serious lesson on the papacy for the lay-
folk in Germany, he closed his treatise with an
entertaining parting shot:

I can see clearly that if I were to permit these
crude heads their presumptions, in the end
even the bath maids would write against me!
I only ask that whoever wants to get at me
should be armed with Scripture. What good
does it do when a poor frog puffs itself up?
Even though he bursts, he will never be like
an ox.[15]

Luther even used humor to tackle his old
enemy Cardinal Albrecht of Mainz, whose
abusive indulgences traffic in 1517 had
spawned Luther's *Ninety-Five Theses*. Albrecht
had used the profits to "buy" his highest
ecclesiastical title from Rome. But in 1521
he again promoted indulgences as rewards
for viewing a new collection of relics in the

newlybuilt cathedral in Halle, inviting his political neighbors, including Luther's "boss" Frederick the Wise, to urge the faithful to take advantage of the new blessings.

Luther heard about this scheme while he was in hiding at the Wartburg Castle and penned a polemical tract, *Against the Idol at Halle.* He sent it to his friends and colleagues in Wittenberg for publication. No one expected anything from Luther's pen since rumors had it that the Wittenberg reformer was dead after his condemnation by church and state in 1521. But Luther was under the protection of Frederick the Wise, who had arranged his secret stay "in the lands of the birds" and on his "Patmos."[16] During a secret visit to Wittenberg Luther agreed with his friends and the Saxon court to wait with the publication of his outburst; but he would send a letter to the cardinal demanding a withdrawal of the indulgences. If he refused, he would attack him in public with the tract on the "idol." The court jester now appeared in the guise of a prosecutor. "If the idol [the sale of indulgences] is not taken down," Luther wrote, "my duty towards divine doctrine and Christian salvation is a necessary, urgent and unavoidable reason to attack publicly Your Electoral Grace (as I did the pope)...and to show to all the world the difference between a bishop and a wolf."[17]

Albrecht's response was quick and surprisingly polite: "I am more than willing to show you grace and favor for Christ's sake, and I can well bear fraternal and Christian punishment."[18] The cardinal had humbled himself before the fearless heretic! But—just to make sure—Luther incorporated his tract on the "idol at Halle" in a less tempered treatise on the Roman hierarchy.[19] Albrecht kept his promise and left Luther alone, but sent a wedding gift of twenty gulden to Luther's bride Catherine; she kept the money despite Luther's objections.[20]

Luther not only tackled his opponents from his exile at the Wartburg but also jested with students when he returned to Wittenberg disguised as a knight. Two students told about their encounter with a knight at the Black Bear Inn in Jena. The knight wore breeches, a doublet, and a red hat; his hand rested on a sword and he was reading a book. The knight invited them for a drink and they discussed the situation in Wittenberg. He advised them to study the original biblical languages if they should decide to become priests. The two students told him that they hoped to meet the professor who had started the reform movement. They suspected that he was not a knight because his book was the Hebrew Psalter. After the knight had paid their bill, he told them to greet Professor Jerome Schurf from "the one who is to come." When they finally arrived in Wittenberg and presented

letters of recommendation to the theological
faculty, they met Luther—he was the knight in
the inn![21]

When the reform movement gained
momentum, Luther turned his attention to the
German nobility, including the emperor, when
he discovered that the "ecclesiastical nobility,"
the German bishops, and the pope appeared
unwilling to deal with abuses and to institute
reforms. He boldly asked the German nobility to take charge of reforms as "emergency
bishops" (*Notbischöfe*) until there would once
again be a faithful church in Germany. Luther
made this plea in the guise of a court jester:

Perhaps I owe my God and the world
another work of folly. I intend to pay my
debt honestly. And if I succeed, *I shall for
the time being become a court jester.* And if I
fail, I still have one advantage—no one need
buy me a cap or put scissors to my head [the
monk's cowl serving as the jester's cap]. It
is a question of who will put the bells on
whom [that is, who is the bigger fool]. I must
fulfill the proverb, "Whatever the world does,
a monk must be in the picture, even if he
has to be painted in." More than once a fool
has spoken wisely, and wise men have often
been arrant fools. Paul says, "He who wishes
to be wise must become a fool" [1 Cor. 3:18].
Moreover, since I am not only a fool, but
also a sworn doctor of Holy Scripture, I am
glad for the opportunity to fulfill my doctor's
oath, even in the guise of a fool.[22]

Luther submitted a long list of ecclesiastical abuses that the new "emergency bishops" should either abolish or reform. When he described the abuse of the cult of the saints, he joked, "My advice is to let the saints canonize themselves."[23] Moreover, he was quite disturbed that many of his supporters talked about an insurrection against the tyranny of the church and the princes who shared it. He told his supporters with humorous humility that the name "Luther" must never be associated with such an insurrection:

In the first place, I ask that men make no reference to my name; let them call themselves Christians, not Lutherans. What is Luther? After all, the teaching is not mine [John 7:16]. Neither was I crucified for anyone. St. Paul, in 1 Corinthians 3[:22], would not allow the Christians to call themselves Pauline or Petrine, but Christian. How then should I—poor stinking maggot-fodder that I am—come to have men call the children of Christ by my wretched name? Not so, my dear friends; let us abolish all party names and call ourselves Christians, after him whose teaching we hold.[24]

Although some German political leaders seemed honest and just with their subjects, Luther did not trust them all. Luther mocked those among the nobility who claimed to obey the emperor yet fleeced the poor behind the mask of "Christian obedience." They claimed to be obedient to the emperor, but if the emperor were to take their castles they would resist him:

> But when it comes to fleecing the poor or venting their spite on the word of God, it becomes a matter of "obedience to the imperial command." Such people were formerly called scoundrels; now they have to be called obedient Christians princes. Still they will not permit anyone to appear before them for a hearing or to defend himself, no matter how humbly he may petition.... Such are the princes who today rule the empire in the German lands. This is also why things are necessarily going so well in all the lands, as we see![25]

"A wise prince is a mighty rare bird," Luther declared, "and an upright prince is even rarer. They are generally the biggest fools or the worst scoundrels on earth."[26]

Luther used his "office" of court jester to expose tyrannical power. But he also suffered from it, having been labeled a heretic by the church and a demagogue by the state. As a specialist in biblical studies, he looked for consolation in the Bible and, when the whirlwind of politics almost swept him away, he found inner peace in knowing that God was his partner in strife: "The more they rage against me, the more he strengthens and extends my cause—without any help or advice from me—as if he were laughing and holding their rage in derision, as it says in Psalm 2[:4]."[27]

As a scholar and educator Luther knew that solid reform must be based on good education. That is why he tried hard from the very beginning of his reform movement to change public opinion in favor of public schools—again with a sense of humor: "When I was a lad they had this maxim in school: It is just as bad to neglect a pupil than to despoil a virgin." The purpose of this maxim was to keep the schoolmasters on their toes, for in those days no greater sin was known than that of despoiling a virgin."[28]

Since he was Germany's best-known outlaw, he could not attend the Diet of Augsburg in 1530. He instead spent his days in the Coburg Castle. Nervous and bored, Luther let his mind wander and compared the birds he observed at his hideout—the "kingdom of the birds"—with the political assembly of the emperor and the princes:

> They are like an army of sophists and Cochlaeans [disciples of his enemy John Cochlaeus] assembled here from all the world, so that I may come to know their wisdom and kindness and learn to appreciate their useful service in the kingdom of the flesh as well as in the kingdom of the spirit.[29]

Luther wrote to his friend George Spalatin: "It is not you people alone who are traveling to a diet, for we, too, arrived at a diet as soon as we parted from you, so we overtook you by far. Therefore our journey to the diet has not been prevented, only changed."[30] Then Luther described what he called "the diet of jackdaws": They assemble under the open sky; they show contempt for foolish luxury; and they act in unison, whether for the sake of food or in song. In short, they know much better how to conduct a diet than the nobles assembled at Augsburg. Luther added a word game based on the Latin and German names for "jackdaw"—*monedula* and *Dohle.*

> If they found a fair interpreter they would derive sufficient glory and praise from [their] very name *Monedula* if it were taken to mean *man Edel*, or *Edelman* ["nobleman"] if you turn the words around. However, at this point begins an affront to your diet, for your *Edelmoni* [Latin plural for "nobleman"] excel too much through *monedulana* virtues [the thievish nature of jackdaws].[31]

Such doodling and joking helped Luther in his loneliness. "This suffices for a joke," he told Spalatin, "but [it is] a serious and necessary joke which should chase away the thoughts seizing me, if I can repel them."

Luther was quite aware of his public image as a reformer and potential martyr. He knew that his reform movement had moved Europe to the brink of war, and that military action might soon accompany the more peaceful, yet still violent, war of words. Although he did not like war, he wrestled his way through to the conclusion that a Lutheran defensive war against an unjust emperor and a political pope was right. In a treatise entitled *Martin Luther's Warning to His Dear German People* (1531), he jests about his power:

> Nothing better could happen to my person than that the papists devour me, tear me, or bite me to pieces, or help me out of this sinful, mortal bag of maggots in any other way. No matter how angry they are, I will say to them: "Dear Sirs, if you are angry, step away from the wall, do it in your underwear, and hang it around your neck!"[32]

Luther knew how to mix laughter with mortal danger, and he was able to wrap the mantle of humor around tough demands. While lecturing on his favorite epistle—Galatians—in the midst of political turbulence, Luther calmly told his opponents on the side of Rome that all issues would be resolved through one single concession. His statement is witty yet also deadly serious:

> All we aim for is that the glory of God be preserved and that the righteousness of faith remain pure and sound. Once this has been established, namely that God alone justifies us solely by His grace through Christ, we are willing not only to bear the pope aloft on our hands but also to kiss his feet.[33]

This was the word of a tested court jester; and it was not a joke, though it sounded like one.

Luther knew that everything depended on a consensus on "justification"—it was not yet on the ecumenical card in the serious game for Christian unity. It would take almost half a millennium to produce a "Joint Declaration on the Doctrine of Justification between Lutherans and Catholics."[34]

Luther played his court jester role once even for an official visitor from Rome. Traveling to Wittenberg in 1535 to meet the diabolical heretic in person, the papal nuncio Vergerio sought to promote a council of Catholic bishops to deal with the growing schism. The Saxon court arranged the meeting for 7 November. Luther changed his clothes for the meeting; he wanted to appear as a well-to-do gentleman of leisure, also much younger than he was. He got shaved and wore youthful clothes: a dark double doublet with satin sleeves over which he wore a short, fur-lined coat made of serge, a light woolen material. In addition, he wore a heavy gold chain and several rings. His outfit gave the impression that he was much younger than fifty-two. Vergerio spoke later of Luther's lively black eyes, which suggested that he might have been possessed by demons. During the conversation, Luther bragged about his marriage to a nun who bore him five children, hinting that the oldest son might continue his work of reform.

Luther had his pastor John Bugenhagen with him. As they were driven to the electoral castle for the meeting, Luther joked, "Here they go, the German pope and Cardinal Pomeranus [derived from Pommerania, Bugenhagen's native territory], the tools of God." Luther played the role of a crude German and asked Vergerio whether they knew him in Italy only as a drunkard. When they discussed the council, Luther assured Vergerio that he would be there if invited. Vergerio left convinced that Luther's cause had been overestimated and that the reformer was just a mentally unstable crude German.[35]

Luther treated his old enemy Archbishop Albrecht of Mainz in a similar yet much more satirical way. It was the third time that the two giants, as it were, met for one more test of power. Luther had first attacked him indirectly in the *Ninety-Five Theses* (1517), then compelled him in 1521 to stop another attempt to grant indulgences through an exhibit of relics. At that time, Luther made Albrecht the target of mocking satire. The archbishop had stayed in the background and did not get involved in the struggle between Wittenberg and Rome. But he seemed to be addicted to relics as a means to offer salvation to those who, like he, believed that there was a link between the remains of dead saints and living members of the church, eager to find an easy way to appease an angry God.

In 1542, the cardinal exhibited his large collection of relics, once again offering indulgences on the basis of solemnly viewing them. Luther decided to mock the cardinal rather than openly attack him. He composed a pamphlet and published it without identifying the author: "New Pamphlet from the Rhine."[36] The pamphlet noted that part of the money collected at the exhibition would be used to provide wrappings for the old relics so that they would not have to freeze in their old ones. In addition, newly discovered relics would be exhibited with a special indulgence offered by Pope Paul III. The new relics included:

- a nice section from Moses' left horn [Exod. 34:29, Vulgate Bible: "His face was horned from the conversation with the Lord"],
- three flames from the burning bush on Mount Sinai [Exod. 3:3],
- two feathers and an egg from the Holy Spirit,
- a remnant of the flag with which Christ opened hell,
- a large lock of Beelzebub's beard, stuck on the same flag,
- one half of the archangel Gabriel's wing,
- a whole pound of the wind that roared by Elijah in the cave on Mount Horeb [1 Kings 19:11],
- two ells [about ninety inches] of sound from the trumpets on Mount Sinai [Exod. 19:16],
- thirty blasts from the trumpets on Mount Sinai,
- a large heavy piece of the shout with which the children of Israel tumbled the walls of Jericho [Josh. 6:20],
- five nice strings from the harp of David, and
- three beautiful locks of Absalom's hair, which got caught in the oak and left him hanging [2 Sam. 18:9].

The author concluded by sharing a tip received from a friend in high places: Archbishop Albrecht had willed a trifle of his pious, loyal heart and a whole section of his truthful tongue to the existing collection, and whoever paid one guilder at the exhibition would receive a papal indulgence remitting all sins committed up to the time of payment and for ten more years, thus giving the people of the Rhineland a unique opportunity to obtain a special state of grace. Luther revealed himself as the author after the pamphlet had been widely circulated.

Waggish Polemics

Once Luther felt liberated from the fear of an angry God, he also felt free to deal with his adversaries on all levels of communication. Frequently, he even signed his letters after October 31, 1517, as "Friar Martin *Eleutherius*" (Greek for "the liberated one").[37] His liberation is also evidenced in his dealings with intellectuals and church leaders who had become his adversaries. He was free to choose from an arsenal of literary weapons to defend himself, without any anxiety about his success. Luther felt that he only needed to be faithful, not successful, in communicating God's unconditional promise of love and salvation in Christ.

Luther enjoyed, to be sure, the progress of the reform movement he had begun. But he was convinced that God's power, not human means, would justify the end. Luther only wanted to make sure that his stance would be understood, even though it may not be appreciated. So when an opponent tried to offer a serious refutation, based on evidence, Luther responded in kind if the evidence was solid. But when adversaries attacked his person, offered irrelevant arguments, or just picked a fight, Luther counterattacked with salvos ranging from waggish polemics to scatological character assassination. As a popular biographer of Luther put it, "Luther delighted less in muck than many of the literary men of his age; but if he did indulge, he excelled in this as in every other area of speech."[38]

Luther's literary feud of 1521 with the Leipzig theologian Jerome Emser (1477–1527) is a case in point. At issue was the understanding of church and ministry in four literary exchanges. Emser identified himself through a coat of arms—a shield and helmet adorned with a goat; the coat of arms appeared on the title pages of his treatises. He provoked Luther's response because he had called Luther's reformatory writings "un-Christian." The titles of Luther's responses already indicate their tone: 1) *To the Goat in Leipzig*; 2) *Concerning the Answer of the Goat in Leipzig*; 3) *Answer to the Hyper-Christian, Hyper-Spiritual and Hyper-Learned Goat Emser in Leipzig—Including Some Thoughts Regarding His Companion, the Fool [Thomas] Murner [a Franciscan from Strasbourg who sided with Emser]*; 4) *Dr. Luther's Retraction of the Error Forced Upon Him by the Most Highly Learned Priest of God, Sir Jerome Emser.*[39] Already Luther's first response reveals his waggish polemics:

> If I had called you a goat, my Emser, you would certainly have written a book or two about it, swamping me with all kinds of lies, slander, and invective, as is your custom. But since you have described yourself as a goat in such glaring letters that everyone must see it, and since you threaten no more than to butt, saying, "Beware, the goat will butt you," I trust I may as well receive you as a goat with your own favor and grace.... But I think I detect your real reason for writing. I shall disregard the fact that you are doing so presuming a skill and intelligence your own conscience undoubtedly denies you. I shall clearly demonstrate this to you when you finish butting and when it is my turn to clip the horns of the goat.[40]

When Emser responded with a treatise entitled *To the Bull in Wittenberg*, threatening Luther with the condemnation of the church, Luther was quick to retort:

> My goat Emser, too, has made horrible threats to butt and has sharpened long spears, short daggers, and swords. The great bloody war was waged on the poor paper, which thus increased the supply for the privy and the dispensary. Even such an honor is too great

for the un-Christian lies, blasphemies, and perjuries which were made against God's holy word.[41]

Luther's polemics also reveal his eschatological perspective, which does not permit final theological solutions regarding the church and its authority. Its structure and leadership may vary in history. The Western Roman church, with the pope as its head, must change because the pope claims to have the full power of Christ on earth. As a theologian, Emser should know the danger of a "realized eschatology," that is, the notion that there is no longer any difference between temporal and eternal power. Luther tells Emser that the eternal Christ is the true head of the church, not the temporal pope.

> Even if the pope should become equal to other bishops, which will not happen until the Last Day (for Christ himself has to remove this enemy of his whom we could not reform), it would not remove the church's head, as Emser lies. He thinks he has won the point that the pope is the head of the church; he has a long way to go. Christ is the head of the church. The pope is often a heretic and knave.[42]

Luther ended the controversy by repeating his main argument (that there is a common priesthood of believers), but clothing it in the form of a retraction: whatever else is said about the priesthood should be retracted in favor of the biblical saying, "You are a royal priesthood" (1 Peter 2:9). Since Emser does not deny this saying, there is an ironic agreement between the two authors:

> For since all Christians are called priests when he says, "You are a royal priesthood," and since it is also to be understood in the sense of the physical priesthood [Emser's term], which is consecrated and tonsured, as swordsman Emser teaches and constructs, we have to confess that all Christians are undoubtedly such physical priests. Otherwise, we are heretics and the devil's property, as Emser threatens.[43]

Although Emser responded with yet another treatise, Luther remained silent. Still, he kept his sense of irony. After his condemnation by church and state in 1521, he signed his writings under the title "ecclesiastic," as if he still was a priest and theologian in good standing.[44] That is why Emser wrote a pamphlet entitled, *Against the Ecclesiastic, Falsely So Called, and True Arch-Heretic Martin Luther.* Luther kept his cool:

> Now that I am deprived of my titles through papal and imperial disfavor and my bestial character is washed away with so many bulls that I need never be called either Doctor of Holy Scripture or some kind of papal creature, I am almost as shocked as an ass who has lost its bag.[45]

He published his own bull against the papacy, which was in Luther's mind the true heresy.[46] The papacy with all its pomp and circumstance is the advertisement with which the devil traps the world:

> The world wants to be fooled. If you wish to catch many robins and other birds, you must place an owl or a screech owl on the trap or lime-rod, and you will succeed. Similarly, when the devil wants to trap Christians, he must put on a cowl, or (as Christ calls it) a sour, hypocritical expression [Matt. 6:16]. Thus we stand in greater awe of such owls and screech owls than of the true suffering, blood, wounds, death, and resurrection, which we see and hear of in Christ, our Lord, endured because of our sin. So we fall, in throngs and with all our might, away from our Christian faith and into the new holiness, that is, into the devil's trap and lime-rod. For we always must have something new. Christ's death and resurrection, faith and love, are old and just ordinary things; that is why they must count for nothing, and so we must have new wheedlers (as St. Paul says [2 Tim. 4:3]).[47]

The devil always tempts naïve believers to mistake a megachurch with its institutional trimmings for the real holy church of God. So "when the devil saw that God built such a holy church, he was not idle, and erected his chapel beside it, larger than God's temple."[48] Luther saw in the papal church God's wrath before the Last Day;[49] and in his own final days Luther directed his satirical, scatological polemics against the papacy as the most abusive institution of his time.

While he was working on his final blast against the papacy,[50] the reformer shared his view with a broad audience in a series of ten satirical caricatures produced by the artist Lucas Cranach in woodcuts with Latin and German commentaries by Luther. The first tablet shows the origin of the papacy by a she-devil whose anus gives birth to the pope and the cardinals; three furies care for newborn "antichrist." The second and third (double) tablets depict a papal council in Germany: one shows the pope riding a pig and holding filth in his hand, which the pig is sniffing (Germany must eat the filth offered by the pope). The other tablet depicts a donkey playing a bagpipe (the pope as incompetent theologian and interpreter of Scripture). The fourth shows the execution of a nobleman through the pope, disclosing the gratitude of the popes towards emperors for yielding such power to Rome. The fifth tablet shows the pope with his foot on the neck of Emperor Frederick I (known as "Barbarossa" or "red beard," 1152–1190) to illustrate papal tyranny. The sixth tablet shows the hanging of the pope and cardinals, with their tongues nailed to the gallows because of their slander; devils receive their souls. The seventh and most popular image shows the papal throne in the jaws of hell and the pope as the antichrist (it is also on the title page of Luther's treatise). Finally, there are tablets with the pope being ridiculed by peasants who expose their hind ends to him; or the pope being an earthly idol used by peasants as a commode.[51]

Luther addressed Pope Paul III as "Most Hellish Father"[52] and as "Holy Madam Pope Paula III."[53] When Rome rejected any interference of the emperor in arranging a General Council to deal with the new reform movement, Luther mocked the pope:

Gently, clear Pauli, dear donkey, don't dance around! Oh, dearest little ass-pope, don't dance around—dearest, dearest little donkey, don't do it. For the ice is very solidly frozen this year because there was no wind—you might fall and break a leg. If a fart should escape you while you were falling, the whole world would laugh at you and say, "Ugh, the devil! How the ass-pope has befouled himself!" And that would be a great crime of lese majesty [mutilated Latin *crimen laesae majestatis*, "a royal crime"] against the Holy See in Rome, which no letters of indulgence or "plentitude of power" [*plenitudo potestatis*, the canonist doctrine of the papal prerogative] could forgive. Oh, that would be dangerous! So consider your own great danger beforehand, Hellish Father. ...If I should die meanwhile, may God grant that someone else make it a thousand times worse, for this devilish popery is the last misfortune on earth, nearest to that which all the devils can do with all their might.[54]

Luther also displayed his waggish polemics on the sensitive subject of the interpretation of the Lord's Supper. Rationalists like the Swiss reformer Ulrich Zwingli had interpreted the word "is" in Christ's institution of the sacrament ("This *is* my body") as "signifies." Thus the true presence of Christ in the Lord's Supper was denied. "Now a sow cannot be a dove," Luther commented, "nor a cuckoo a nightingale. This proud devil treats Scripture any way he pleases."[55] He claimed his "jester's privilege" to speak jokingly about Holy Scripture and a holy sacrament.[56]

Luther also engaged in waggish polemics against opponents on the Protestant side, such as Ulrich Zwingli who denied the real presence of Christ in the Lord's Supper. A colloquy in Marburg (1529) between Zwingli's group and Luther's team yielded no reconciliation. Luther knew that there would be no consensus on the interpretation of the Lord's Supper. Before the meeting of the two dialogue teams he wrote with chalk on the table, "*hoc est meum corpus*" ("this is my body") and covered the words with a table cloth. At the height of the debate he lifted the tablecloth and said, "It is written...." The two teams departed in a shallow peace!

Luther's serenity was tested severely in his exchange with the great humanist Erasmus of Rotterdam (1469–1536) on the enduring theological question whether or not the human will is free to decide in the matter of salvation. Erasmus tried to defend such freedom; Luther denied it. But he disagreed with the most formidable philosopher of his time; Erasmus represented the best and brightest form of humanism, a philosophical movement that based truth on solid historical evidence and challenged many claims of the church. Moreover, Erasmus had provided the first Greek edition of the New Testament, the most effective source of Luther's biblical studies. But when Luther encountered the haughty argumentation of the great philosopher, who always claimed to be right, he once again used his serene humor to show that there was more smoke than fire in the Erasmian argumentation.

Luther sought to defuse, as it were, the great philosopher's argumentation already in the Preface of his response to Erasmus, the treatise *On the Bondage of the Will*. The words cut the ground from Erasmus's feet with waggish false praise:

> I yield you a palm such as I have never yielded to anyone before; for I confess not only that you are far superior to me in powers of eloquence and native genius (which we all must admit, all the more as I am an uncultivated fellow who has always moved in uncultivated circles), but that you have quite damped my spirit and eagerness, and left me exhausted before I could strike a blow.

There are two reasons for this: first, your cleverness in treating the subject with such remarkable and consistent moderation as to make it impossible for me to be angry with you; and secondly, the luck or chance or fate by which you say nothing on this important subject that has not been said before. Indeed, you say so much less, and attribute so much more to free choice than the Sophists [a contemptuous term for "scholastic theologians"] have hitherto done (a point on which I shall have more to say later) that it really seemed superfluous to answer the arguments you use. They have been refuted already so often by me, and beaten down and completely pulverized in Philip Melanchthon's *Commonplaces* [*Loci communes*]—an unanswerable little book which in my judgment deserves not only to be immortalized but even canonized. Compared with it, your book struck me as so cheap and paltry that I felt profoundly sorry for you, defiling as you were your very elegant and ingenious style with such trash, and quite disgusted at the utterly unworthy matter that was being conveyed in such rich ornaments of eloquence, like refuse or ordure being carried in gold and silver vases.[57]

At the end of his long response to Erasmus Luther again strikes him with his club of waggish polemics. Praising Erasmus's promotion of the study of classical languages and literature, Luther delivers his final blow: the "venerable master" does not know what he is talking about because the subject matter is too much for him.

> But God has not yet willed or granted that you should be equal to the matter at present at issue between us. I say this, as I beg you to believe, in no spirit of arrogance, but I pray that the Lord may very soon make you as much superior to me in this matter as you are in all others. There is no novelty in it, if God instructs Moses through Jethro [Exod. 18:13f.] and teaches Paul through Ananias [Acts 9:10f.].[58]

2
Wit and Witness

Divine Comedy in the Bible[1]

When Luther let the Bible penetrate his
anxious, guilt-ridden life as a young monk,
priest, and professor, he discovered the only
text about the laughter of God: "He who sits
in the heavens laughs; the Lord has them in
derision" (Ps. 2:4). Luther argued in his lectures
that God's laughter hides divine wrath from
the follies of humankind: "He laughs because
He grants time for repentance."[2] Luther's
spiritual struggle had taught him that he was
loved and protected by God, and was thus on
God's side when he was attacked. This passage
gave Luther the ability to laugh at his enemies
because they are insignificant in the light of
God's power in Christ, who leads his followers
through this world to the heavenly city. That is
why Christ tells his disciples, "Be of good cheer,
I have overcome the world" (John 16:33).

Focused on Christ, Luther could stay serene
and cheerful in the face of the overwhelming
odds that threatened his life and his reform
movement. No one, of course, will ever be as
serene as God is in the midst of the spiritual
storms in the world. But a true doctor of theology
will always continue to learn new skills of
healing like a true doctor of medicine.

We should, then, become accustomed to these storms in which a Christian must live and continuously dwell, and we should withdraw to the shadows and lay hold of the invisible. Then it will come about that we shall laugh at the fury of the Turk, the popes, tyrants, sects, heretics, and of all the adversaries of Christ's kingdom, as a comical spectacle. He who is able to do this everywhere and always is a true doctor of theology. But neither Peter nor Paul nor the other Apostles could always do this. Therefore we must confess that we also are only students and not doctors in this art, although we do not even deserve the name of students, since when God laughs, we are either angry or vexed.[3]

Luther admitted that God's laughter made him nervous. But since he was called by God to live and work by faith in Christ alone, he could claim that he learned from the Bible to laugh rather than despair over the incongruities of life in all its various relationships. With the author of Ecclesiastes, Luther could say that "all is vanity" (Eccles. 1:2) while sharing Paul's conviction that nothing can separate believers from the love of God in Christ (Rom. 8:38–39). Thus Luther gained the significant theological insight that biblical faith is linked with a humor that discloses a glimpse of eternal joy beyond death, something of the image of God within human life.

Luther was a professor of biblical studies who loved to work on Genesis in the Old Testament and on Galatians in the New

Testament. His commentaries are laced with humor. His humor is revealed in a gigantic commentary on salvation history from the creation of the world to the death of Joseph,[4] and in his lectures on Galatians (1519 and 1535). Galatians was as dear to him as was his wife; he called the epistle "My Katie von Bora."[5] Luther's commentaries on Genesis and Galatians show how he combined the witness of Holy Scripture with wit: "the keen perception and apt expression of surprising, incongruous, subtle, or hilarious relations between phenomena, ideas and words."[6]

Genesis

Although Luther used traditional medieval principles of exegesis, he was more often than not "above" the interpreters, probably fancying himself to be like God in Ps. 2:4. A sampling of his work shows his humorous serenity. Commenting on the creation of the world in six days, he warned his readers of the existing exegetical confusion regarding "heaven" in Gen. 1:6 ("Let there be a dome in the midst of the waters, and let it separate the waters from the waters"):

> Ambrose [340–397] and Augustine [354–430] have rather childish ideas. Therefore I commend Jerome [348–420], *who maintains complete silence on these topics.* Some call the crystalline heaven "watery" because they

believe that it represents the waters of which Moses is speaking here, and that they were added to the eighth sphere to keep it from going up in flames because of the excessive motion. But these are childish ideas. Rather than give approval to those inept thoughts, I for my part shall confess that I do not understand Moses in this passage.[7]

When Luther reached the stories about the creation of small animals, he encountered medieval commentators who adopted Aristotle's view of science and contended that dung beetles were brought into being from the impact of the sun on horse manure. Luther had doubts about that. When he lectured on the creation of whales ("great sea monsters"—Gen. 1:21), he turned his attention to beetles and other small animals, like mice:

Aristotle states that certain animals are produced by their like, others by their unlike. Thus mice belong to the kind produced by their unlike, because mice originate not from mice alone but also from decay, which is used up and gradually turns into a mouse. If you should ask by what power such a generation takes place, Aristotle has the answer that the decayed moisture is kept warm by the heat of the sun and that in this way a living being is produced, just as we see dung beetles being brought into existence from horse manure. *I doubt that this is a satisfactory explanation. The sun warms; but it would bring nothing into being unless God said by His divine power: "Let a mouse come out of the decay."*

> Therefore the mouse, too, is a divine creature and, in my judgment, of a watery nature and, as it were, a land bird; otherwise it would have the form of a monster, and its kind would not be preserved. But for its kind it has a very beautiful form—such pretty feet and such delicate hair that it is clear that it was created by the Word of God with a definite plan in view. Therefore here, too, we admire God's creation and workmanship.[8]

The mouse—a tiny flying whale?

Luther imagined Adam as a kind of superman before the Fall—tall, extremely intelligent and handsome, surpassing all other living creatures. "I am fully convinced that before Adam's sin his eyes were so sharp and clear that they surpassed those of the lynx and the eagle."[9] Luther offered his own ideas about the Fall: Satan was jealous of Adam's gifts, and so he tempted Eve—"perhaps at noon"—to desire even more than God had already provided for her and Adam in paradise. It is the enduring temptation to be greedy and selfish.

> So it is wont to be to this day. Where the Word of God is, there Satan also makes it his business to spread falsehood and false teaching; for it grieves him that through the Word we, like Adam in Paradise, become citizens of heaven. And so he successfully incites Eve to sin.[10]

In Luther's mind, Adam and Eve were the first members of the church who had ignored

God's first admonition about the tree of knowledge (Gen. 2:16). "If they had not fallen into sin," he lamented, "Adam would later have transmitted this single command to all his descendants. From it would have come the best theologians, the most learned lawyers, and the most expert physicians."[11]

When he commented on Adam's long life of 930 years, he called his time a "golden age." He believed people back then lived a healthy life, were moderate in their diets, responsible to other family members and happy with each other: "Thus that age was truly a golden one. In comparison with it our age hardly deserves to be called an age of mud."[12]

Luther's imagination and wit moved into high gear in his comments on the story of Noah and the flood. Other interpreters had been particularly concerned about the size of the ark, the number of animals it accommodated, and the space provided for them on three decks (Gen. 6:15). Luther created his own arrangements:

> It is likely that Noah and the birds occupied the uppermost part, the clean animals the middle part, and the unclean animals the lowest, although the rabbis would maintain that the lowest was used for putting away the manure. I myself believe that the manure was thrown out, perhaps through the window.... We shall put aside countless other questions. [But what] was the nature of the air in the ark, since that mass of water, especially when it went down, gave off a great and pestilential stench?[13]

The rainbow as a sign of God's covenant with Noah (Gen. 9:12–16) prompted Luther to comment on the speculations of philosophers regarding the nature of rainbows: "A philosopher, I am sure, will figure out something, for he will regard it as a disgrace not to be able to give reasons for everything. But he certainly will never persuade me to believe that he is speaking the truth."[14] Luther himself was quite willing to call such "phenomena" as rainbows, flying dragons, and leaping goats, the "antics of demons in the air" obeying God's will.[15]

Luther rejected allegorical interpretations as fabrications used to explain anything for selfish purposes. Switching once again to irony, he mentioned especially the allegories used by the pope, claiming that the papal office is the sun and secular authority is the moon, deriving its light from the sun (as Pope Innocent III had claimed in 1198).[16]

Luther used the stories of Abraham and Lot to comment on the confused relationship between law and love in Germany. The proverbial critique targets vocations that make high claims: "Hence the German proverbs about the young doctor of medicine who needs a new cemetery, the jurist who recently took over a public office and starts wars all over the place, and the young theologian who fills hell with souls."[17] Luther mocks those who claim to be experts because they know some details. Using ancient Greek for the interpretation of the New Testament had become fashionable. Luther mocks that habit: "If someone is able to write four Greek words to explain one Psalm, he is puffed up with his knowledge as if by yeast."[18]

Sodom's sin (Gen. 19:1-28) is used by Luther to point to the continual lack of hospitality, revealing the smugness of evil and the swiftness of divine punishment: the most respectable citizens of Sodom violated the law of hospitality with their demand for sexual pleasure. "They not only showed no courtesy towards the guests, they did not allow the tired men to rest even for an hour in someone else's house."[19] Luther felt that the same is true also about respect for God's power. When Lot told his sons-in-law about the imminent destruction of the city, they thought it was a bad joke (Gen. 19:14). Luther's comment includes a story about the Pope who condemned him: Leo X.

> Thus the story is told about Pope Leo that he once invited two philosophers to dinner. One of them discussed the immortality of the soul; the other discussed its mortality. When, after a long, hot debate, the pope had to decide which of the two had spoken more correctly, he said to him who had defended the immortality of souls: "To be sure, you seem to be stating facts; but your opponent's discourse creates a cheerful countenance." Epicureans are in the habit of doing this; over against the clear truth they draw conclusions that suit the flesh and reason.[20]

The selfish arrogant power of worldly rulers, among them the pope, seeks flattering entertainment at the expense of truth. Luther linked this tale with another one, involving a selfish, ambitious nun.

> She took delight in her contemplations and carefully kept away from the other nuns, lest her thoughts be hampered. When she thought she was dressed in a golden robe and adorned with a golden crown and thus, like a bride at her marriage, sat there delighted and rejoiced, the rest of the nuns discovered the mockery; for instead of a crown on her head they saw cow dung. She dreamed that this was a golden crown.[21]

Lot's sexual sins with his daughters (Gen. 1:31–33) impelled Luther to muse, "Why does Moses state that Lot was not aware of it?" He offers his own answer: "Lot had been absorbed in the height of excitement and for this reason does not remember afterwards what he did."[22] Moreover, he was drunk. What about the motives of Lot's daughters? "They devised this plan not because they are stirred by lust but because of their extraordinary compassion for the entire human race."[23] Luther explained that there were no more men on earth to preserve the human race, and so the daughters made their father drunk in order to suppress his moral judgment regarding this unusual deed. Luther then offers this commentary on the story, including his own opinion about the irony of salvation history:

You will ask: "But why does God permit His own to fall in this manner?" Although we are not at liberty to inquire too eagerly into God's doings, yet here the answer is easy. God wants us to be well aware of our feebleness, lest we lapse into smugness. Thus Lot and his saintly household had seen the sins of the people of Sodom and had rightfully abominated them, but what happens to them now? The people who are so saintly pollute themselves with abominable incest, something which hardly ever happened among the people of Sodom or at least did not happen commonly.[24]

Luther rejected the suggested interpretation that Lot was given a potion by his daughters to numb his moral sense. Luther contended that the region where Noah lived produced excellent wine; that is why Moses "called it a paradise of God. Therefore Lot became drunk not because he drank wine so excessively, but because his perturbed mind could not tolerate such excellent wine."[25] Luther loved to speak of the paradox of sinners and saints. When even the biblical saints become too smug, as the story of Lot suggests, God moves in to teach these lessons!

Luther's serenity created a spiritual freedom that sometimes eliminated the historical distance between him and his biblical heroes. Regarding the famous story of the sacrifice of Isaac, Luther imagined himself standing next to Abraham and Isaac at the terrible moment when the father is told by God to kill his son as a sacrifice (Gen. 22:9). Moses must have omitted an emotional exchange between father and son, Luther commented. Isaac must have been amazed and could not have been obediently silent. He must have reminded his father that he was the offspring to whom future kings and prophets had been promised, and Luther has him say, "God gave me to my mother through a great miracle. How then will it be possible for the promise to be fulfilled if I have been killed? Nevertheless, let us first confer about this matter and talk it over."[26] When Abraham's wife Sarah died, he must have delivered a beautiful eulogy, Luther suggested. He admired her. After all, she accompanied her husband through thick and thin and was a saintly woman. "It is easy for me to believe that in her hundredth year she was just as beautiful as she was in her twentieth," Luther wrote. "In Holy Scriptures no other matron is so distinguished."[27]

Rebecca is for Luther an example of obedience without procrastination because she did not yield to the temptation to stay home (Gen. 24:55–61). Luther coins a proverbial phrase in her honor: "The Holy Spirit does not bestow His gifts on procrastinators; He bestows them on those who are prompt, ready and alert."[28]

Keturah, Abraham's second wife (Gen. 25:1), prompted Luther to state his opinion of husbands. He lists four classes: 1) those who

marry and have children; 2) those who marry
for the sake of avoiding fornication and to be
chaste; 3) those who marry only for pleasure
and want to have a pleasant life with a pretty
young girl; and 4) those who marry old ladies
for their wealth. Luther wishes these latter bad
luck: "May God give them the cup of suffering."[29]
A good marriage, on the other hand, should be
enjoyed: "We are permitted to laugh and have
fun with and embrace our wives, whether they
are naked or clothed," just as Isaac fondled his
wife Rebecca (Gen. 26:8).[30]

Luther comments on the story of Rachel's
devious theft of household gods (Gen. 31:33–
35): "Here Satan is aiming at Rachel's throat."[31]
God and Satan play with people, according
to Luther, exemplified in the story of Jacob
wrestling with God (Gen. 32:24). Jacob could
have had all kinds of ideas about it, but he did
not, Luther said. He then told the story of a
young man confessing his lust for women to
a hermit. The old hermit told the young man:
"You cannot prevent the birds from flying
over your head. But let them only fly and do
not let them build a nest in the hair of your
head. Let them be thoughts and remain such;
but do not let them become conclusions."[32]

Galatians

When Luther lectured on Galatians he presented the epistle as Paul's best witness of
"justification by faith alone." But Paul also

warns of Satan's continual attempt to steal this chief article of faith and substitute the doctrine of justification by works and the authority of human traditions. Luther warned that such teachings always seem to be more reasonable. Reason easily becomes a source of self-righteousness, Luther declared, and he made his point by using an analogy: "As soon as reason and the Law are joined, faith immediately loses its virginity."[33] He presents the distinction between law and gospel in a monologue, comparing the function of the law with the work of a donkey:

> When your conscience is completely terrified by a sense of sin, you will think of yourself. "At the moment you are busy on earth. Here let the ass work, let him serve and carry the burden that has been laid upon him; that is, let the body and its members be subject to the Law. But when you ascend into heaven, leave the ass with his burdens on earth; for the conscience has no relation to the Law or to works or to earthly righteousness. Thus the ass remains in the valley; but the conscience ascends the mountain with Isaac, knowing absolutely nothing about the Law or its works but looking only to the forgiveness of sins and the pure righteousness offered and given in Christ."[34]

In another witty analogy, Luther compared living by faith alone to a bride who is alone with her bridegroom, Christ. "But later on, when the bridegroom opens the door and comes out, then let the servants return to take care of them and serve them food and drink. Then let works and love begin."[35]

Luther praised Paul for using "most delicious language" in telling the Galatians that he died to the Law through the Law in order to live with God (Gal. 2:19). "Here Paul is the most heretical of heretics,"[36] Luther commented— because he refused to live by the law. So one can say to the devil,

> "Mr. Devil, do not rage so. Just take it easy! For there is One who is called Christ. In Him I believe. He has abrogated the Law, damned sin, abolished death, and destroyed hell. And He is your devil, you devil, because He has captured and conquered you, so that you cannot harm me any longer or anyone else who believes in Him."[37]

According to Luther, those who say they love the law do not know what they are saying. Like "a thief or a robber who loved his prison and his shackles," such a person "would be...out of his mind.[38]

Luther's regular preaching at the Town Church in Wittenberg and sometimes in the Saxon countryside also has its share of humor. Luther sometimes preached long sermons and singled out listeners who fell asleep or coughed too much. His expository preaching was often quite entertaining. For many years, the popular Luther biographer Roland Bainton performed excerpts from Luther's Christmas sermons (on Luke 2:1–7) at the Yale Divinity School. An annually increasing audience could hardly stop laughing. Focusing on the poor conditions under which the baby Jesus was born, Luther brought the biblical story to the hearts and minds of his listeners in Wittenberg:

There are many of you in this congregation who think to yourselves: "If only I had been there! How quick I would have been to help the baby! I would have washed his linen. How happy I would have been to go with the shepherds to see the Lord lying in the manger!" Yes, you would! You say that because you know how great Christ is, but if you had been there at that time you would have done no better than the people of Bethlehem. Childish and silly thoughts are these! Why don't you do it now? You have Christ in your neighbor. You ought to serve him, for what you do to your neighbor in need you do to the Lord Christ himself.

The birth was still more pitiable. No one took her [Mary's] condition to heart. ...There she was without preparation: no light, no fire, in the dead of night. No one came to give her customary assistance. The guests swarming in the inn were carousing, and no one attended to the woman. I think myself if Joseph and Mary had realized that her time was so close she might perhaps have been left in Nazareth. And now think what she could use for swaddling clothes—some garment she could spare, perhaps her veil—certainly not Joseph's breeches which are now on exhibition in Aachen.[39]

Facetious Pastoral Care

Throughout his busy life as a teacher, pastor, and celebrity, Luther gave lots of advice—and at times even took it! He always responded to queries or calls for help; and he offered his pastoral care and counsel on the basis of his theological convictions, usually in the context of a rational diagnosis of a case in question, but sometimes also with the force of uncritical emotions when his theological convictions were challenged.

An example of careful, yet unwise advice was Luther's 1540 approval of the bigamy of the powerful "Lutheran" nobleman Philip of Hesse (he was the head of the Lutheran military Smalcald League). The unhappily married Philip had entered a bigamous marriage with a young lady at his court after intensive discussions with lawyers and theologians, especially Luther. Bigamy was prohibited by law. But Luther acted like a priest who may in rare circumstances recommend something illegal under the seal of private confession. Since marriage was not a sacrament but a secular order of God, according to Luther's biblical view, he had no basic objections to bigamy as a way to avoid divorce. After all, the Bible allowed even polygamy in the Old Testament and accepted a "Turkish marriage" (in accordance with Islamic law that allowed men to marry more than one woman).

But since Luther was aware of the solid Christian medieval tradition of monogamous marriage, without the permission of divorce, he advised Philip in private confession to keep the second marriage a secret. However, Philip's sister discovered her brother's deed, and the story quickly spread. Luther had advised Philip to lie about the bigamy in case it should be discovered; such a lie was approved in medieval pastoral care as a "necessary lie" to protect the absolute secrecy of private confessions. Luther seemed to be naïve about the power of gossip and when the bigamy became known he felt betrayed. "Had I known that [Philip violated the oath of secrecy], indeed no angel should have persuaded me to give such advice."[40]

Nevertheless, Luther had no real regrets or feelings of guilt. Such spiritual accidents occur on the difficult track of pastoral care and pastors have to live with them. As Luther put it: "If I should now defend what I have said or done years ago, especially in the beginning, I would have to worship the pope."[41] In the final analysis, Luther contended, one must leave such matters to God; otherwise the devil will take over and make things worse. But Luther admitted in a conversation with his colleague and friend Philip Melanchthon that "the dirt still falls on both of us!"[42]

Luther's pastoral care and advice exhibits the freedom of living in eschatological time, when nothing is absolutely sure and true except the Word of God in Christ. How Luther used this conviction in seemingly difficult cases of pastoral care is illustrated in his advice regarding changes in public worship.

Liturgy is always a sensitive matter involving symbols, emotions, and rites. When Elector Joachim II of Brandenburg introduced a new liturgy in 1539, his young Lutheran pastor, George Buchholzer, thought that the liturgy was very "un-evangelical." He wrote to Luther that the Elector ordered the use of Roman vestments and a procession with the eucharistic elements around the church (as was done in the medieval church at the Feast of Corpus Christi). Luther responded in two letters, one to the Elector and the other to the pastor. He criticized the Elector for introducing devilish customs such as the carrying around of eucharistic elements.[43] He advised Buchholzer to concentrate on word and sacrament; but also encouraged him to use various liturgical ornamentations as long as the consciences of the parishioners were not burdened.

> Why don't you, for heaven's sake, march around wearing a silver or gold cross, as well as a scull cap and a chasuble made of velvet, silk or cotton? If your superior, the Elector, thinks that one cap or one chasuble is not enough, then put on two or three, like Aaron, the High Priest, who wore three coats, one on top of the other, and they all looked wonderful [Lev. 8:7]....If your Electoral Excellency

thinks one procession is not enough, marching around with singing and with bells, then do it seven times, just as Joshua did in Jericho with the children of Israel. They shouted and blew their trumpets [Josh. 6:4–7]. Perhaps your Electoral Excellency might even jump around and dance in front of all the people with harps, drums, cymbals and bells, just as David did before the ark of the covenant on its way to Jerusalem. I completely approve of such things, as long as they are not viewed as necessary for salvation, or binding to consciences.[44]

Luther closed the letter with the remark that the *way* of human worship "is a free thing and not a divine mandate."[45]

In some situations, Luther accomplished more with sheer humor than with serious piety. This is demonstrated in his dealings with his servant Wolfgang. Wolfgang loved to attract birds with food and trap them with a primitive net that he put up near Luther's home, the Augustinian monastery. He then sold the birds to people who liked to cage them or eat them as a delicacy. Luther, who hated to see birds suffer, could simply have ordered Wolfgang to stop his sport and business enterprise. Instead he sent him a pamphlet, entitled "A Complaint of the Birds. Addressed to Dr. Martin Luther Concerning His Servant Wolfgang Sieberger."[46] The style and content of the pamphlet resembled a legal complaint with the birds accusing Wolfgang of depriving their liberty.

We, the plaintiffs—blackbirds, thrushes, finches, linnets, gold-finches and other good and honorable birds who must travel this fall via Wittenberg—want Your Kindness to know that one called Wolfgang Sieberger, your servant, as has been credibly reported to us, is guilty of a vagrant crime. Motivated by great anger and hatred against us, he has purchased some old worn-out and damaged nets at an expensive price in order to build a trap for finches. Moreover, he is not only after our friends, the finches, but deprives us of the God-given right to fly and collect some grain. He wants to take our lives and limbs, even though we have done nothing to threaten him and do not deserve such malicious treatment.

The birds then plead with Luther to make Wolfgang stop these forays against them, or at least to make him stay in bed until 8:00 a.m., so that the birds can fly over Wittenberg safely. If, however, Luther should not succeed in stopping Wolfgang, then the birds would have no choice but to undertake countermeasures.

If he does not [stop], but continues to threaten our lives, we shall plead with God that He might make him catch frogs, grasshoppers and gnats during the day and that he be covered with lice, fleas and bedbugs at night so that he forgets about us and no longer impedes our free flight.

The complaint concludes with the suggestion that Wolfgang trap sparrows and rats instead, for they steal from people, whereas good birds only take the few grains left on the ground after the harvest. At the bottom of the document is the official place of issue: "In our heavenly seat under the trees with our usual seal of feathers." Wolfgang understood the broad hint and quit trapping birds.

Luther again resorted to wit when in 1535 he sought permission from the Saxon authorities to stay with his parishioners when Wittenberg was once again threatened by bubonic plague. The Saxon authorities urged Luther to move to Jena where the program of the university would continue until the danger had passed. Luther refused to move. In a letter to Elector John Frederick he stated his reason: the long nose of the official representative of the Saxon court in Wittenberg, District Governor Hans Metzsch, had given him sure-fire clues that the plague would not strike Wittenberg: "My weathervane is the District Governor Hans Metzsch who has so far had a real buzzard-nose concerning the plague. Even if his nose were five ells under the earth, he would still smell it. But since he is staying, I can't believe that the plague will come."[47] Luther then told the Elector that the plague had struck only two households so far and that the students were pleased because they liked to see their gear contaminated so that they did not have to study—their bags swollen, their books colicky, their pens suffering from a rash, their papers rheumatic, and their ink moldy. Luther concluded the letter with a serious note, asking for medical assistance. In 1527, when the plague had struck Wittenberg, he had given advice that government officials and pastors should not flee from the plague but stay and care for the afflicted. Since it is the devil's work, one must be of good cheer, get away from oneself, and mock the devil, who uses the plague to frighten souls out of their faith in Christ.

> "Get away, you devil, with your terrors! Just because you hate it, I'll spite you by going the more quickly to help my sick neighbor. I'll pay no attention to you: I've got two heavy blows to use against you: the first one is that I know that helping my neighbor is a deed well-pleasing to God.... Should not my dear Christ, with his precepts, his kindness, and all his encouragement, be more important in my spirit than you, roguish devil, with your false terrors in my weak flesh?...
> The second blow against the devil is God's mighty promise by which he encourages those who minister to the needy. He says in Psalm 41 [:1-3], "Blessed is he who considers the poor."... What should terrorize us or frighten us away from such great and divine comfort?[48]

Luther also used his facetious pastoral care on his spouse, Catherine von Bora ("Katie"), when she worried too much about her husband's journey to his native Eisleben in the final year of his life. Luther loved and respected her. He admired her strength and skill as the manager of his large household, addressing her frequently with "Dear Lord" or "Dear Sir" in letters.[49] But when she sent him letters worrying about his stay in Eisleben during a very bad winter, Luther sent her a letter disclosing his teasing yet caring humor.

> I thank you very kindly for your great worry which robs you of sleep. Since the date that you [started to] worry about me, the fire in my quarters, right outside the door of my room, tried to devour me; and yesterday, no doubt because of the strength of your worries, a stone almost fell on my head and nearly squashed me as in a mouse trap. For in our secret chamber [the toilet], mortar has been falling down for about two days; we called in some people who [merely] touched the stone with two fingers and it fell down. The stone was as big as a long pillow and as wide as a large hand; it intended to repay you for your holy worries, had the dear angels not protected [me]. [Now] I worry that if you do not stop worrying the earth will finally swallow us up and all the elements will chase us. Is this the way you learned the *Catechism* and the faith? Pray, and let God worry. You have certainly not been commanded to worry about me or about yourself. "Cast your burden on the Lord, and he will sustain you."[50]

Luther did not mention the devil as the cause of the accident on the toilet, as he usually did. But his letter is a typical expression of his facetious pastoral care, which certainly included his dear Katie.

Gallows Humor

Ever since Luther was saved from spiritual despair about an angry God, he gained an inner strength and freedom to face *Anfechtung* and even death with humor. Knowing about the happy end of Christian life with Christ at the end of all human time created a powerful serenity in his career as a reformer. He was able to distance himself from impatient judgment and actions, taking time for a reality check, as it were. Thus Luther learned that moral action must be done for the neighbor in need without any expectation of eternal personal benefit. Christ is the only mediator "who gave himself a ransom for all" (1 Tim. 2:6). In the light of the Last Day, good deeds are good in themselves, not because they are done by Christians or other religious people. Consider this lifesaving action:

> Someone is drowning and is pulled out of the water by three swimmers: a Christian, a Communist and a Hindu. They proudly proclaim that their religious convictions motivated their good deed. The action was the same, though the confession of faith made it a Christian, a Communist, and a Hindustani deed. "It makes no difference who saved me," said the survivor. "I just wanted to be pulled out of the water!"

Any similar testimony about facing fear and death in retrospect can reflect serenity exhibited as gallows humor, in the sense of "humor that makes fun of a very serious or terrifying situation."[51] Consider this joke involving a survivor of the *Titanic*:

> Hundreds of passengers who had jumped overboard in the middle of the night were floating in the ocean, some holding on to pieces of furniture and other floating debris. An elderly lady, still dressed for dinner in expensive jewels and a fancy hat, clung to a wooden board. After some lengthy drifting, she was joined by one of the ship's kitchen chefs, identified by his hat. "Dear Ma'am," he said, almost without breath, "are you alright?" "Of course I am alright," she said calmly. She then added: "By the way, my dear, what would have been the soup du jour tomorrow?"

Luther exhibited this kind of gallows humor centuries earlier, in an age of much superstition, fear of dying, and fear of divine punishment. When he became very tired in his busy life, he complained about all the work, but added a humorous twist: "I have worked with all my might. For one person I've done enough. All that's left is to sink into my grave. I'm done for, *except for tweaking the pope's nose a little now and then.*"[52]

A year before he died, a friend sent Luther an Italian pamphlet with a German translation, entitled *An Italian Lie Concerning Dr. Martin Luther's Death.*[53] An anonymous author had recorded "a terrible and unheard of miraculous sign which the blessed God has shown in the shameful death of Martin Luther." The "sign" depicted Luther's request to have his body placed upon an altar and worshipped after his death. The request, however, could not be granted, argued the author, because Christ himself intervened, handing Luther's body over to the devil in an awful and noisy ceremony. Only "a sulfurous smell" remained near the empty tomb where Luther had been laid.

Luther had the pamphlet published with a brief comment that he had enjoyed reading the lie about his death. He expressed his hope that the pope and the papists might still be turned away from the devil, but left the matter of Luther's death in God's hands. When the messenger who had brought the pamphlet asked Luther to tell the world that he was still alive, Luther penned an epitaph, "written from my grace."

I, Dr. Martin Luther, testify herewith in my own hand that I am of one mind with the devil, the pope, and all my enemies, for they wish to rejoice over my death. I begrudge them their joy from the bottom of my heart and would willingly have died...but God was not yet ready to sanction such joy. He will do this, however, sooner than they think, and it will be their misfortune, for they will then say, 'Would that Luther were still alive!' This is a transcript in German, Greek, Latin, and Hebrew from my grave.[54]

Luther also loved to tell the story of a "saint" named Agnes who was honored by the church for her cheerful attitude as a martyr. He saw himself mirrored in this story when he lectured on Gen. 48:21, where Jacob talks about his death with Joseph.

> Faith begins life and has it in itself, and we who believe have this beginning, that even when we feel death, we nevertheless do not fear it as others, who are tormented by an evil conscience and grow pale even when the word "death" is mentioned, feel it. But the godly and saintly martyrs despise death and laugh at it. Thus when Agnes was being carried off to prison and torture, she said that she felt just as if she were being led to a dance. What, I ask, was the source of such great courage on the part of the maiden? She was not afraid. She did not tremble. No, she exulted as though she were being summoned to a most sumptuous feast. This was no Epicurean contempt of death; it was true wisdom and understanding, because of which she concluded that life was very close to her. *Therefore she laughed at the devil and death and regarded them as a joke, because for her death had been swallowed up through life. This is the theology we teach.*[55]

Luther contrasted gallows humor with the German custom of doing "a gallows repentance" (*eine Galgenreue*)—a "deathbed repentance." It is a false repentance, focusing on the harm done to oneself, not on the fear of divine punishment. Joyful humor is replaced with a joyless self-righteousness. Luther saw such a false repentance symbolized in Esau, who cheated his brother Jacob out of his inheritance (Gen. 27:33–36):

> The Germans call it "a gallows repentance," namely, when I repent in such a way that I am not ashamed of having offended God but am ashamed because I have done harm to myself. Such a repentance is very common, and I myself have often repented in this manner; and I felt sorry that I had done something foolishly, unwisely, and with harm. I was more ashamed of the foolishness and harm than of the sin, than of the guilt or offense. But to feel sorry only for the harm that has been done is a repentance of which God has no knowledge. Indeed, even our own hearts have no knowledge of it, as is evident in the case of Esau; for he does not say: "Now I realize that I have sinned. Why did I offend God by selling my birthright? Now I shall gladly do without the blessing, provided that God forgives me this sin." This would have been a true repentance, with which he would have been concerned about appeasing God on account of the sin that had been committed. For true repentance looks at God's wrath on account of sin.[56]

The Esau-types of Christians stage a hypo-critical "pity party" for themselves to avoid punishment; they never truly repent of their sin. Luther saw this tradition of false repen-tance grounded in the self-righteous excuses offered by Adam and Eve after the Fall: Adam blames Eve for his sin; Adam blames even God, because he had given Eve to him; and Eve blames the serpent (Gen. 3:12–13).

Luther was able to laugh in terrifying situations because he placed all his trust in God and thus no longer tried to sweat out of his *Anfechtungen*:

> This is the work and skill of God, to correct and amend what had been ruined by Jacob's error. He can make evil matters good when we have spoiled and harmed matters. And so, in the great infirmity characteristic of human affairs, not even the saints can be without many great lapses. Certainly, I have often done many things imprudently and foolishly, concerning which I was much disturbed later. Nor was I able to see how I might work my way out and extricate myself from matters that were being hampered by my folly. But the Lord found a means and a way that the error might be corrected.[57]

Such trust in God as the power of the future gives Luther the serenity to look death in the eye with a smile. Speaking about the suffering of Israel in Egypt, he views himself as part of the ancient history of the people of God.

> These are works of God which are not understood unless they are fulfilled and completed. In the meantime, however, while they are being carried out, they cannot be grasped except by faith alone. For it is necessary simply to hold fast to this: "I BELIEVE

IN GOD THE FATHER ALMIGHTY, Maker of heaven and earth, etc."

In the same manner, when I am about to depart from this life, I support myself with this consolation that I believe in God's Son. And yet I am buried; I am eaten by worms; I am consumed by the most foul rottenness, as Job says (Job 17:14)....Here I do not discern God's plan, that although I die and rot away, I must at some time be revived...[as] God has promised....But all these things are done in a hidden manner, and so the wonderful concealment of God must be borne and endured....With our God this is as if it had already taken place. It certainly comes to pass![58]

Good cheer by anticipation!

Again and again, Luther relied on his experience of a gracious God who alone has the power to overcome the problems of the world grounded in evil, sin, and death. Living by faith in Christ alone means to replace, as it were, the contracted arteries of a downcast heart with new life-giving arteries; instead of trying to breathe harder with a sad heart, one yields to the promise of a happy heart. Commenting on Ecclesiastes 9:8—"Let your garments be white"—Luther puts these words into Solomon's mouth:

"You are living in the midst of vanity. Therefore enjoy life, and do not let yourself come to ruin through your indignation, but drive the grief from your mind. *You cannot mock the world more effectively than by laughing when it grows angry. Let it be enough for you that you have a gracious God. For what is the malice of the world in comparison with the sweetness of God?"* [Solomon] is not urging a life of pleasure and luxury characteristic of those who do not sense this vanity, for that would be putting oil on fire; but he is speaking of godly men, who sense the vexation and troubles of the world. It is their downcast hearts that he wants to encourage. It is to them that he recommends merriment.[59]

Luther intensified his gallows humor into mockery when he and his reform movement were threatened with extinction in 1525. Luther had been hunted as a heretic and demagogue after the Diet at Worms (1521); "Lutheran" knights had lost their battle with the emperor (1523); and the peasants' revolt against feudal landlords ended in the peasants' bloodbath (1525). In the midst of these calamities Luther decided to get married to an apostate nun!

I almost believe and think that it is because of me that the devil is making such a mess in the world, in order that God might vex the world. Well, if I get home [from a trip to Eisleben] I shall prepare for death with God's help, and await my new lords, the murderers and robbers, who tell me they will not harm anyone. They are like the highway robber who said to the good coachman: "I shall do you no harm, but give me all you have and drive where I tell you; and if you don't you will die!" Beautiful innocence! How magnificently the devil decorates himself and his murderers! But I would rather lose my neck a hundred times than approve of and justify the peasants' actions; may God help me with his grace to do this. If I can manage it, before I die I will still marry my Katie to spite the devil, should I hear that the peasants continue. I trust they will not steal my courage and joy.[60]

At another difficult time, when Luther was hiding at the Coburg Castle during the fateful Diet of Augsburg (1530), Luther put his mind on music (perhaps even playing his lute) and composed an antiphon. He sent it to Louis Senft, a leading composer of the time. The survival of the Lutheran reform movement was at stake in Augsburg where their *Confession* was submitted to the emperor. The Wittenberg professor felt again the threat of death:

Indeed, I hope that the end of my life is at hand; the world hates me and cannot bear me, and I, in turn, loathe and detest the world; therefore may the best and [most] faithful shepherd take my soul to him. And so I have already started to sing this antiphon and am eager to hear it arranged. In case you should not have or know it, I am enclosing it here with the notes; if you wish you can arrange it–perhaps after my death.[61]

Luther suffered from kidney stones, gallstones, frequent insomnia, headaches, and angina pectoris. In his final year he wrote to an old friend and colleague, Nicholas von Amsdorf: "Farewell in the Lord, my Reverend Father! Both of us are old, perhaps in a short while we will have to be buried. My torturer, the [kidney] stone would have killed me on St. John's Day, had God not decided differently. I prefer death to such a tyrant."[62]

Luther spent his final days counseling two feuding noblemen in his native town of Eisleben. He was not in good health and joked about the joy of dying in his letter to one of the noblemen, Count Albrecht of Mansfeld: "I am ready to give up eight days, one way or the other, for this matter—though I have very much to do—so that I may lie down in my coffin with joy."[63]

Luther liked to summarize his difficulties with the image of Satan riding through his head, looking for a spa.[64] If the devil tried to stay in his head to create confusion, Luther told his dinner guests, he found a way to resist him with scatological language.

I am of a different mind ten times in the course of a day. But I resist the devil, and often it is with a fart that I chase him away. When he tempts me with silly sins I say, "Devil, yesterday I broke wind too. Have you written it down on your list?"...I remind myself of the forgiveness of sin and of Christ and I remind Satan of the abomination of the pope. This abomination is so great that I am of good cheer and rejoice, and I confess that the abomination of the papacy after the time of Christ is a great consolation to me.[65]

When the first edition of Luther's massive German writings appeared in 1539, Luther's gallows humor made him the critic of his own works.

> Although it is not my will...I have no choice but to let them risk the labor and the expense of this project. My consolation is that, in time, my books will lie forgotten in the dust anyhow, especially if I (by God's grace) have written anything good. ["I am no better than my fathers" (1 Kings 19:4).] He who comes second should indeed be the first one forgotten.

Luther then said that the Bible is the only book that is important because "it turns the wisdom of all other books into foolishness." There is indeed a time, Luther tells other writers, when "you will not only despise the books written by adversaries, but the longer you write and teach the less you will be pleased with yourself." Finally, Luther offers this mocking advice:

> If, however, you feel and are inclined to think you have made it, flattering yourself with your own little books, teaching, or writing, because you have done it beautifully and preached excellently; if you are highly pleased when someone praises you in the presence of others; if you perhaps look for praise, and would sulk or quit what you are doing if you did not get it—if you are of that stripe, dear friend, then take yourself by the ears, and if you do this in the right way you will find a beautiful pair of big, long, shaggy donkey ears. Then do not spare any

expense! Decorate them with golden bells, so that people will be able to hear you wherever you go, point their fingers at you, and say, "See, See! There goes that clever beast, who can write such exquisite books and preach so remarkably well." That very moment you will be blessed and blessed beyond measure in the kingdom of heaven. Yes, in that heaven where hellfire is ready for the devil and his angels.[66]

Quite an autobiographical preface for a world-class author!

3

Smiling through the Mean Meantime

Penultimate Thinking

It is said in Germany that Saxons have an inherent sense of humor, perhaps because they have had a long, varied history ever since the first ruler of a European super-power, Charlemagne (742–814), converted them to Christianity. Luther once remarked that "all nations are simple in comparison with Saxons" who adopt the vices of other nations, as did his enemy, Cardinal Albrecht of Mainz, whom he accused of becoming as sly as Italians: "Beware of an Italo-German! For as soon as a German learns epicureanism in Italy and adopts the hellish art, he becomes more deceitful than Italians."[1]

Luther added a theological dimension to the ethnic wit of Saxons: the biblical sense of life as a mean meantime before the Last Day makes true, faithful Christians smile about the adversities; indeed, they can laugh at them because the anticipated joy of a future without sin, evil, and death outweighs all earthly anxiety. In this sense, eschatological humor is an integral ingredient of a spiritual and theological discipline which, like the training of an athlete, prepares for the final run to victory. In other words: since the ultimate is constantly in sight, the penultimate is no longer deadly serious. Here Luther adopts the stance of the apostle Paul who linked the power of love with the anticipation of the Last Day:

> Love never ends. But as for prophecies, they will come to an end; as for tongues, they will cease; as for knowledge, it will come to an end. For we know only in part, and we prophesy only in part; but when the complete comes, the partial will come to an end.... For now we see in a mirror, dimly, but then we will see face to face. (1 Cor. 13:8–10, 12)

Viewed in the context of the divine promise of a happy end, earthly life shares such happiness even though it is still tied to the tough problem of survival in the midst of a fallen world. Luther, therefore, called for a view of earthly life guided by the infinite promise of God and not only by finite human reason.

> What a Christian has is in fact something very large and infinite, but according to his view and sense it is very small and finite. Therefore we must not measure this by human reason and sense; we must measure it by another circle, that is, by the promise of God; just as He is infinite, so His promise is infinite, even though meanwhile it is enclosed in these narrow limits and in what I might call the Word of the center. Now we see the center; eventually we shall see the circumference as well.[2]

According to Luther, reasoning is limited to the things before the last things, the penultimate; speculations about the last things, the ultimate, are useless because the ultimate belongs to the realm of divine promise, known only through faith in Christ. Thus, during the interim between Christ's first and second advent, eschatological humor replaces theological speculations about God without Christ, along with the establishment of unchanging moral rules. Proper "God-talk" (or "theology," from the Greek *theologia*, "knowledge" and/or "teaching about God") and "God-walk" (ethics) must avoid what is "supernatural" (*super naturam* in Latin, "above nature"), or "metaphysical" (*meta physis* in Greek, "behind nature"). As Luther told the philosopher Erasmus who claimed that human beings are endowed with a "natural" freedom to decide for or against their salvation:

> God does many things that he does not disclose to us in his word; he also wills many things which he does not disclose himself as willing in his word. Thus he does not will the death of a sinner, according to his word; but he wills it according to that inscrutable will of his. It is our business, however, to pay attention to the word and leave that inscrutable will alone, for we must be guided by the word and not by that inscrutable will. After all, who can direct himself by a will completely inscrutable and unknowable? It is enough to know simply that there is a certain inscrutable will in God, and as

to what, why, and how far it wills, that is
something we have no right whatever to
inquire into, hanker after, care about, or
meddle with, but only to fear and adore.[3]

Early in his life, Luther was deadly afraid
of the wrath of the hidden God because he
never could do enough to appease a God
who punishes sinners.

I was troubled...by the thought of what God
would do with me, but at length I repudiated
such a thought and threw myself entirely
on his revealed will. We can't do any better
than that. The hidden will of God can't be
searched out by man....We have enough to
learn about the humanity of Christ, in whom
the Father revealed himself. But we are fools
who neglect the revealed Word and the will of
the Father in Christ and, instead, investigate
mysteries which ought only be worshiped.
As a result many break their necks.[4]

Luther calls proper Christian theology
"practical" because its foundation is Christ,
whose death is appropriated to us by faith.[5]
"Speculative" theology ignores this foundation and engages in rational explanations:

We're not content with that which we can
understand and insist on disputing about
something higher, which we can't possibly
understand and which our Lord God doesn't
want us to understand. That's the way human
nature is. It wishes to do what is forbidden;
the rest it ignores and then starts asking,

Why? Why? Why? This is what happens when philosophy is introduced into theology. When the devil went to Eve with the question Why? the game was up. One should be on one's guard against this. It's better to fall on one's knees and pray an Our Father. This will help more. "Dear Lord God, protect us from the devil, and also from ourselves!"[6]

Luther contends that the problems of earthly life are created by selfishness and the human desire to be in charge, "to be like God" (Gen. 3:5). The way of the serpent seems more attractive than the way of Christ; the sin of pride is stronger than love of neighbor. This is the continual conflict between the ultimate, the eternal majesty of God, and the penultimate, earthly life under the condition of sin. Since sinful human creatures cannot do anything about their salvation from sin other than become faithful disciples of Christ, Luther assigns absolute priority to the penultimate phase of Christian existence. For God is disclosed in his humanity in Christ. Proper theology must focus on the way God deals with sin and salvation, with justification by faith and not by human efforts.

The proper subject of theology is man guilty of sin and condemned, and God the Justifier and Savior of man the sinner. Whatever is asked or discussed in theology outside this subject, is error and poison.... The issue here is not this physical life—what we should eat, what work we should undertake, how we should rule our family, how we should till the soil.... The issue here is the future and eternal life; the God who justifies, repairs, and makes alive; and man, who fell from righteousness and life into sin and eternal death.[7]

Luther learned the hard way, through the pain of spiritual *Anfechtung*, not to pursue a *speculative* theology dealing with the ultimate, the last things—life after death, or the nature of the hidden God. He became convinced that such a theology denigrated, if not abandoned, the foundation of the Christian faith: God's clear promise, in word and sacrament, that by God's incarnation in Jesus Christ, the Second Adam, the fallen creation will be healed. That is why all theology is for Luther a lifelong undertaking to "learn Jesus Christ, 'and Him crucified' (1 Cor. 2:2)."[8] He put it most succinctly in the *Smalcald Articles*, his theological testament:

That Jesus Christ, our God and Lord, "was handed over to death for our trespasses and was raised for our justification" (Rom. 4:25).... Now because this must be believed and may not be obtained or grasped otherwise with any work, law, or merit, it is clear and certain that this faith alone justifies us,... nothing in this article can be conceded or given up, even if heaven and earth or whatever is transitory passed away.[9]

Luther once tried to explicate in Latin the chief article of justification in a scholastic fashion. The effort was entitled *On Justification (de loco justificatione)*. He called it a "rhapsody."[10] He had already composed a ballad on "justification," to be sung as a hymn. Titled "Dear Christians, Let Us Now Rejoice," the hymn has God dialogue with his Son (in ten verses!) on how to save the world from sin.[11] According to Luther, poetry, music, and humor are better means to express God's love of the sinner in Christ than logic. The gift of faith in the mean meantime of earthly life before the Last Day offers an unusual freedom to be more doxological than logical, more free to live a joyful life with smiling serenity. It creates a mental distance from evil, sin, and death; this distance should be celebrated, not academically argued. That is why Luther said,

> We can mention only one point (which experience confirms), namely, that next to the Word of God, music deserves the highest praise. She is a mistress and governess of those human emotions—to pass over the animals—which as masters govern men or more often overwhelm them. No greater commendation than this can be found—at least not by us. For whether you wish to comfort the sad, to terrify the happy, to encourage the despairing, to humble the proud, to calm the passionate, or to appease those full of hate—and who could number all

these masters of the human heart, namely,
the emotions, inclinations, and affections
that impel men to evil or good?—what more
effective means than music could you find?
The Holy Ghost himself honors her as an
instrument for his proper work when in
his Holy Scriptures he asserts that through
her his gifts were instilled in the prophets,
namely, the inclination to all virtues, as can
be seen in Elisha [2 Kings 3:15]. On the other
hand, she [music] serves to cast out Satan,
the instigator of all sins, as is shown in Saul,
the king of Israel [1 Sam. 16:23].[12]

There is overwhelming evidence from
Luther's life and work to prove that for him
at least, humor, next to music, was the most
effective way to endure the trials of the
penultimate life. In his way of thinking and
being, smiling, laughing, and even mocking
become the divinely inspired means of
spiritual survival. Knowing of the happy
end at the Last Day, Luther could remain
cheerful in anticipating it. In fact, cheerful
days reminded him of "the dear, sweet Last
Day"—as he wrote to his wife during a trip
filled with earthy happiness, though also
with a heat wave!

Your Grace should know that we are chipper
and healthy here [in Eisenach] (God be
praised), eat like the Bohemians (yet not too
much) and drink like the Germans (yet not too
much)....Also, Master Philip [Melanchthon]
has again been totally restored [from a severe

illness]. God be praised....Here there is such
a heat and drought that it is beyond words
and unbearable [day] and night. Come, O
Last Day. Amen.[13]

Only Germans have not developed a healthy
sense of humor in the face of adversities,
Luther joked; they prefer getting drunk. He,
however, is not such a German, he told dinner guests in a sarcastic comment:

> "One must make the best of the vices that
> are peculiar to each land. The Bohemians
> gorge themselves, the Wends [Slavic settlers
> in Saxony] steal, the Germans swill without
> stopping. How would you outdo a German,
> dear Cordatus, except by making him drunk—
> especially a German who doesn't love music
> and women?"[14]

To Luther, the divine promise of "justification by faith alone" is the final word
of salvation in the penultimate life; it is
the assurance that, through faith in Christ,
believers already experience the end of the
divine judgment of their sin. They live in
Christ, as it were, and no longer have to fear
any judgment while living or dead after the
Last Day. Here Luther adopted the teaching
of Paul that "it is no longer I who live, but it
is Christ who lives in me" (Gal. 2:20).

> Christ and I must be so closely attached
> that He lives in me and I in Him. What a

marvelous way of speaking! Because He lives in me, whatever grace, righteousness, life, peace, and salvation there is in me is all Christ's; nevertheless, it is mine as well, by the cementing and attachment that are through faith, by which we become as one body in the Spirit....Thus Eph. 5:30 says: "We are members of the body of Christ, of His flesh and of His bones," in such a way that this faith couples Christ and me more intimately than a husband is coupled to his wife.[15]

Luther used the biblical analogy of marriage, anchored in deep mutual love, to illustrate the new reality created by faith already in the earthly penultimate life. This new reality grants freedom from fear and punishment and the joy of a new relationship: "If Christ is a bridegroom, he must take upon himself all the things which are the bride's and bestow upon her the things that are his."[16] Luther called this analogy "a most pleasing vision not only of communion, but of a blessed struggle and victory and salvation and redemption."[17] He calls faith the wedding ring, disclosing the new reality of life with Christ. "Thus the believing soul by means of the pledge of faith is free in Christ, its bridegroom, free from all sins, secure against death and hell, and is endowed with the eternal righteousness, life and salvation of Christ its bridegroom."[18] This freedom empowers believers to survive the penultimate mean meantime until the beginning of the ultimate time when sin, evil, and death are no more. But there is still the struggle with evil in the penultimate life. Luther described it in a delightful manner:

> The person who believes in Christ is righteous and holy through divine imputation. He already sees himself, and is, in heaven, being surrounded by the heaven of mercy. But while we are lifted into the bosom of the Father and are clad with the finest raiment, our feet reach out below the garment, and Satan bites them whenever he can. Then the child struggles and cries out, and realizes that he is still flesh and blood, and that the devil is still there and plagues him constantly until the whole man grows and is lifted up out of this wicked and evil world. Thus we are saints and children [of God], but in the spirit, not in the flesh, and we dwell under the shadow of the wings of the mother hen, in the bosom of grace. But our feet must still be washed, and because they are unclean must go on being bitten and tortured by Satan until they they are clean. For you must draw your tiny feet with you under the garment, otherwise you will have no peace.[19]

Christians must focus their mind on the penultimate and not become otherworldly by concentrating on the ultimate. They need the power of a new creation only in this life, not in the next. Whatever the "new heavens and a new earth" may be (2 Peter 3:13), they describe a reality that goes beyond the bounds of reason. "Just as little as babies in the womb know about their arrival [in the world], so little do we know about eternal life."[20] Every Christian "must make sure to keep the Gospel in order to be with the blessed number of those on the right hand of the Lord and blissfully anticipate the Last Judgment."[21] The church, as the gathering around the gospel in word and sacrament, enjoys the presence of Christ, its Lord. Nevertheless, one must move from Sunday to Monday, as it were, still enduring the struggle with evil:

> Now, however, we remain only halfway pure and holy. The Holy Spirit must always work in us through the Word, granting us daily forgiveness until we attain to that life where there will be no more forgiveness. In that life there will be only perfectly pure and holy people, full of integrity and righteousness, completely freed from sin, death, and all misfortune, living in new, immortal, and glorified bodies.[22]

Baptism initiates us into this struggle, with the divine promise of victory. This sacrament "signifies that the old creature in us with all sins and evil desires is to be drowned and die through daily contrition and repentance, and on the other hand that daily a new person is to come forth and rise up to live before God in righteousness and purity forever."[23] The Lord's Supper sustains believers in this struggle, offering the real presence of Christ through the Word, the bread and the wine:

There are so many hindrances and attacks of the devil and the world that we often grow weary and faint and at times even stumble. Therefore the Lord's Supper is given as a daily food and sustenance so that our faith may be refreshed and strengthened and that it may not succumb in the struggle but become stronger and stronger. For the new life should be one that continually develops and progresses.[24]

The Christian mind must face evil, diagnose it and struggle against it with the spiritual gifts of the ultimate in order to survive the penultimate. Individual mystical withdrawal or communal attempts to create the kingdom of God on earth are spiritual pipe dreams, according to Luther. Conflict, on the other hand, is orthodox: "Whoever desires to see the Christian Church existing in quiet peace, entirely without crosses, without heresy, and without factions, will never see it thus, or else he must view the false church of the devil as the real church."[25] In such a situation, Christians must become wise as serpents and innocent as doves, as Jesus told his disciples when they were terrorized in an incredible environment of evil like "sheep among wolves" (Matt. 10:16–25). Luther combined a serpentine sagacity for evil with dove-like, innocent joy of life in Christ.

Even though Christ commands His disciples in Matt. 10:16 to imitate doves in their simplicity, that is, to be sincere and without venom, He nevertheless urges them to be wise as serpents; that is, they should be on their guard against insincere and treacherous people, and they should be cautious, the way a serpent in a fight is said to protect its head with extraordinary skill.[26]

Here Luther agrees (in an entirely different context) with Thomas Jefferson that "the price of liberty is eternal vigilance."

Daily Life before the Last Day

Luther was concerned that the end of the world was near because of signs listed in the Bible: political upheavals caused by insurrection and radical spiritualists (*Schwärmer*), the military advance of the Turks, natural disasters like floods in Germany and elsewhere, and the appearance of the antichrist in the guise of the pope. But he also anticipated, like a child before Christmas, the transition to a new creation that had already created a vision of faith about a life after death. The first Sabbath, described as God's rest from his gigantic work of creation (Gen. 2:3), foreshadowed the final Sabbath. The Mosaic commandment to worship God on the seventh "holy day" and "holiday" (*Feiertag* in German) links Christians with eternal life:

All the things God wants done on the Sabbath are clear signs of another life after this life....To attain it we need the Word and the knowledge of God....The beasts, such as dogs, horses, sheep, and cows, indeed also learn to hear and understand the voice of man; they are also kept by man and fed. But our state is better. We hear God, know His will, and are called into a sure hope of immortality.[27]

Luther singled out his dog "Klutz" (*Tölpel* in German) once as an example of concentration. "Oh, if I could only pray the way this dog watches the meat! All his thoughts are concentrated on the piece of meat. Otherwise he has no thought, wish or hope."[28]

Sundays and holidays, then, should be days of comfort, according to Luther, and reminders of the Christian trek into a new life. This life, however, is still a halfway house, as it were, between sin and salvation:

Now, however, we remain only halfway pure and holy. The Holy Spirit must always work in us through the Word, granting us daily forgiveness until we attain to that life where there will be no more forgiveness. In that life there will be only perfectly pure and holy people, full of integrity and righteousness, completely freed from sin, death, and all misfortune, living in new, immortal, and glorified bodies.[29]

Spiritually serene, though not without anxiety attacks caused by personal illness and events like the peasants' rebellion of 1525, Luther decided to marry an apostate nun, Catherine von Bora. "If I can manage it, before I die, I will still marry my Katie to spite the devil should I hear that the peasants continue. I trust that they will not steal my courage and joy."[30] It was a marriage of inconvenience, as it were. Opponents mocked Luther; his best friend and partner in the reform movement, Philip Melanchthon, was so annoyed that he did not attend the wedding; and supporters were puzzled because their hero was not head over heels in love.

Nevertheless, Luther staged a public scandal and fell in love later; he was forty-two, she was twenty-six. They lived in the Augustinian monastery where Luther had had all his severe *Anfechtungen*. She became a mother of five children, extended Luther's life through a healthy diet, and managed an efficient, yet complex, household. Students and faculty of Wittenberg University, guests of all stripes, and even opponents of Luther's cause praised Katie's partnership with Luther. He himself enjoyed the changed life in the monastery, which the Saxon court had given to him as a parsonage. Luther mused:

> Before I was alone; now there are two. Or in bed, when he wakes up, he sees a pair of pigtails lying beside him which he hadn't

seen there before. On the other hand, wives bring to their husbands, no matter how busy they may be, a multitude of trivial matters. So my Katy used to sit next to me at first while I was studying hard and would spin and ask, "Doctor, is the grandmaster [of the Teutonic Order in Prussia] the margrave's [of Brandenburg] brother?"[31]

Luther's children reminded him of life before the Fall and after the Last Day. When he saw the children at play, he remarked:

Such was our disposition in paradise— simple, upright, without malice. There must have been real earnestness there, just as this boy speaks about God piously and with supreme trust and just as he is sure of God. Such natural playing is best in children, who are the dearest jesters. The affected play of old fools lacks such grace. Therefore little children are the finest mockingbirds and talk naturally and honestly.[32]

Infant Martin's suckling at his mother's breast exemplified for Luther trust in God.

All the demons hate this child, yet the little child isn't afraid of all of them put together. He sucks with pleasure at those breasts, is cheerful, is unconcerned about all his enemies, and lets them rage as long as they wish. Christ said truly, 'Unless you become like children,' etc. (Matt. 18:3).[33]

The sudden death of his teenage daughter Magdalene (little "Lenchen") tested Luther's faith more than any other event in his life. But he yielded to the power of the future marked by resurrection and eternal life: "I am joyful in spirit but I am sad according to the flesh. The flesh doesn't take kindly to this. The separation [caused by death] troubles me above measure. It's strange to know that she is surely at peace and that she is well off there, very well off, and yet to grieve so much!"[34]

Painful illnesses—kidney and gallstones, headaches, insomnia, stomach disorders, and angina pectoris—only reminded Luther that Christians, especially theologians, must struggle with evil in the daily life before the Last Day. But one must fight the devil of disease with the medicine of faith in Christ.

> The devil has sworn to kill me, this I certainly know, and he will have no peace until he has devoured me. All right, if he devours me, he shall devour a laxative (God willing) which will make his bowels and anus too tight for him. Do you want to bet? One has to suffer if he wants to possess Christ. It would be easy indeed for us to triumph if we were willing to deny and calumniate [Christ]. Yet it is written: "Through many tribulations we must enter the Kingdom of God" (Acts 14:22). This is no longer just a word; it has become a reality, and we should act accordingly. Yet He is [here] who along with the tribulation brings about the escape for the faithful.[35]

In addition to his more painful afflictions, Luther at times experienced ringing in the ears and vertigo, probably because of his increasing angina pectoris. But he told dinner guests: "I don't want to find fault with my head. It has faithfully ventured into battle with me. It has deserved my best thanks."[36] Kidney stones almost killed Luther while he attended the meeting of the Lutheran defense league at Smalcald in 1537. He was sent home in a fast-moving carriage, and the lengthy journey over potholes released a kidney stone and saved his life:

> I'm obliged to be stoned to death like Stephen and to give the pope an occasion for pleasure, but I hope he won't laugh very long. My epitaph shall remain true: "While alive I was your plague, when dead I'll be your death, O pope."[37]
>
> After I requested that I be taken away from Smalcald in order that I might not die and be buried there in the presence of that monster [the papal legate Vorstius], I arrived in Tambach, where I drank a little red wine in the inn. Soon afterward by God's grace my bladder was opened, and so I wrote on the wall, 'Tambach is my Phanuel' [cf. Luke 2:36], for the Lord appeared to me there. If I'd died there, my death might have brought complete disaster to the papists, for when I die they'll see what they've had in me.[38]

Luther sometimes survived a tough period of time by grumbling, asking God to endure his physical weaknesses. "For myself I desire a good hour of passing on to God," he told a friend two years before he died.

"I am content, I am tired, and nothing more is in me."[39] A few days before he died, Luther joked about his physical difficulties in a letter to his wife, Katie. After some dizziness caused by an icy wind, he told her:

> But thank God now I am well, except for the fact that beautiful women tempt me so much that I neither care nor worry about becoming unchaste....I am drinking beer from Naumburg which tastes to me almost like the beer from Mansfeld which you praised to me. It agrees with me well and gives me about three bowel movements in three hours in the morning.[40]

Luther used the pulpit to vent his anger about the lack of financial support, but as usual, he used sarcastic humor manifested in benevolent scolding. The problem was the lack of financial support of pastors through the Wittenberg parishioners. He probably hid a smile from his face when he called them "rascals" and threatened to quit preaching to them.

> I hear that you people will not give the collectors anything and turn them away. Thanks be to God that you unthankful people are so stingy with such a contribution and give nothing, but with foul words chased away the deacons. I wanted you to have a good year! I am amazed, and I do not know if I will preach any more, you uncouth rascals.[41]

Disciplined charity, "good works," are part of church discipline, according to Luther; it is a wedge against the devil, especially in the final days before the Last Day. Luther listed the kind of daily living one should avoid as the wiles of the devil: believing in witches, in women who claim to make water, and in other superstitions; the pleasure of bathing in the cold river Elbe because the devil snares people in the forest and in open water (people should bathe at home, Luther advised).[42] He did not mind exposing people who defecate in the street in public view. Luther thought that such people were diabolically shameless and should be stopped; he himself encountered them and denounced the event from the pulpit, together with carrying weapons illegally and taking justice into one's own hands.[43] When the Saxon court issued a mandate in 1531 against heavy drinking, Luther agreed with the new laws, but was reluctant to link them with the proclamation of the gospel. Still, he was convinced that there should be law and order in daily life before the end.

Luther also made some sarcastic comments about men who boasted of their manhood by drinking or showing off their weapons and being loudmouthed; he called them "iron-eaters" who were really only "cowardly boys." On the other hand, Luther allowed preachers to curse in order to defend God's honor![44] He was especially stern with heretics and

Schwärmer who, like the Anabaptists, rejected infant baptism; they must be exposed and cursed when they infiltrate congregations with their false teachings. Luther warned public officials against them.[45]

When all is said and done, Luther contended, the "golden rule" (Matt. 7:12, "In everything do to others what you would have them do to you") should be the "reality check," as it were, for everyone in the daily life before the Last Day. Luther maintained that the rule should apply in all existing walks of life. One should be spiritually lighthearted, but quite serious in the care for a healthy community.

> If you are a manual laborer, you find that the Bible has been put into your workshop, into your hand, into your heart. It teaches and preaches how you should treat your neighbor. Just look at your tools—at your needle or thimble, your beer barrel, your goods, your scales or yardstick or measure—and you will read this statement inscribed on them. Everywhere you look, it stares at you. Nothing that you handle every day is so tiny that it does not continually tell you this, if you will only listen. Indeed, there is no shortage of preaching. You have as many preachers as you have transactions, goods, tools, and other equipment in your house and home. All this is continually crying out to you: "Friend, use me in your relations with your neighbor just as you would want your neighbor to use his property in his relations with you."[46]

In matters such as personal finances and household, Luther left everything in Katie's care. Given his meager income and high expenses, Luther hoped that between Katie and trust in God he and his family would survive (he never collected royalties for his publications or accepted any kind of honoraria). In a humorous summation of his precarious earthly life as the head of a complicated household, the Wittenberg professor offered an account of numerous expenses for the academic year of 1535/36, ranging from foodstuffs to alms for beggars; he entitled it *Amazing Accounting between Doctor Martin Luther and Katie.*[47] But he felt underqualified for the actual accounting. "If I had to take care of building, brewing, and cooking," he joked, "I'd soon die."[48] On the other hand, he was worried about all the work Katie was doing. But all he could think of was to pay her fifty gulden if she would take time out from her many chores and read through the Bible in several months—hardly a time of leisure![49]

Luther put his peculiar, often humorous, stamp on everything he encountered in daily life, like his opinion about the work of farmers on whom he depended as sources for food. His comments appear in the context of his theology of creation as an earthly partnership between God and the human creatures. But one is prone to smile (or feel sad) with modern hindsight when one reads how Luther compared his garden harvest and his vocation as a pastor with the slave labor of the peasants. He told farmers that God gave them a fine creation for their work, just as he, Luther, had a fishpond filled with pike, gudgeon, trout, ruff, and carp with which Katie enriched their dinner table; she, of course, did all the labor in the garden. But when there was a poor harvest, Luther, the pastor, told the peasants that God withdrew the gifts of creation because farmers refused to hear the Word of God in church! Luther was less offensive when he complained that parishioners cheated at certain occasions, like weddings, when they served adulterated wine (adding sulfur) and rancid bread—as Luther himself experienced. "Now they are accustoming us to brimstone and pitch," he commented at his dinner table, "so that we'll be better able to get along in hell."[50]

Luther enjoyed good food and wine, often breaking out in song after a meal and inciting his guests to sing along—occasionally interrupted by noisy children and accompanied by the howling dog Klutz. Luther blamed bad meals without good beer or wine for his stomach problems evident in diarrhea and constipation. "We have nothing to drink," he wrote to his friend Melanchthon while the plague struck Wittenberg. "In the last two days I have had fifteen bowel movements."[51] When he reached the age of sixty, he felt "old, cold, and mutilated" (*alt, kalt ungestalt*). He could pray only, "Thy will be done"—the devil was weary with him and he was weary of the devil.[52]

But Luther never lost his cheer in living with the wonders of God's creation and the expectation of a new creation. Katie's garden was a symbol of divine goodness, yielding vegetables and fruit. When the children enjoyed a peach at the table, Luther said they were a model of joy at the Last Day. Compared with the fruits of paradise, however, a peach was but a crab apple, symbolizing decay of sinful creatures after the Fall:[53]

"How pleasant the trees are! How delightfully green everything's beginning to be! It's like a charming day in May....Ah, would that we could trust God! If God can take such delight in our earthly sojourn, what must it be like in the life to come?"[54]

Two days before his death, Luther scribbled some notes on a piece of paper, wondering how anyone could ever sufficiently grasp historical sources, be it ancient writers before Christ or Holy Scripture. "We are all beggars, that is true," Luther confessed—the final written sentence of his life and work.[55]

Reborn Free

Luther's humor is embedded in his view of time as the final time, ending in the final "little hour" (*Stündelein*).[56] He rediscovered the significance of this biblical view during his decisive spiritual struggle with the question, "How do I find a gracious God?" and its answer, "I find a gracious God by faith alone in Jesus Christ." This answer made Luther feel born again.

The biblical insight that "the righteous live by their faith" (Hab. 2:4; Rom. 1:17) became the leitmotif of Luther's entire life and work. He understood himself to be one free by faith from sin, evil, and death. Such freedom makes believers coworkers with God in a fallen creation, joining the redeeming ministry of Christ in the communication of the "good news," the gospel, announcing the advent of a new creation. Christians are reborn to be free because they believe that the coming of Christ in the final "little hour" determines all of time. It is the moment that—like the ringing of an alarm clock— liberates from sleep to a new day with new tasks. It is the hour appointed by God that gives meaning to all time. Ordinary time is an experience of bondage; the final "little hour" transforms ordinary time into a time of discipleship with Christ who, through word and sacrament, makes believers survive the mean meantime on earth. "In the ['little'] hour God wills the action to be effected, man receives from God a creative freedom to carry the action through against all opposition."[57]

Luther comments on Eccles. 3:1 ("For everything there is a season, and a time for every matter under heaven") and shows the way in which he had learned to understand the dialectic of "ordinary time" and the final "little hour":

> It is not up to us to prescribe the time, the manner, or the effect of the things that are to be done; and so it is obvious that here our strivings and efforts are unreliable. Everything comes and goes at the time that God has appointed.... So the power of God comprehends all things in definite hours, so that they cannot be hindered by anyone....Therefore one should commit things to God and make use of present things, refraining from a lust for future things. If you do otherwise, you will have nothing but affliction.[58]

Not to consider time, Luther contends, leads to the illusion of free choice in everything, including the freedom to accept or reject God's gift of love (the means of overcoming sin, evil, and death). A true awareness of time makes us aware that we do not have a choice when to be born, when to die (though suicide may be a terrible option), or when to get rid of a disease. "Man is not to rack his brain about the future, but live in the hour that has come. That is the same as living in faith, receptive to God who is present now and has something he will do now."[59]

Luther thought that God selects certain people, "wonder men" (*Wundermänner*), to carry out specific divine assignments. They may be believers or nonbelievers, but are usually in a position of leadership, like King David in Israel, King Cyrus in Persia, or Alexander the Great in Greece. Luther liked to use the Roman hero Hannibal (147–183 B.C.E.) as a model of how God chooses people to teach selfish tyrants a lesson. Luther had read the story of Hannibal in the works of the famous Roman statesman and orator Cicero (106–143 B.C.E.). Hannibal was a famous general from the African kingdom of Carthage. After victories against Rome, he retreated to the Seleucian kingdom in Syria where King Antiochus protected him. Hannibal's stay in Syria is the subject of legends that praise his unique talents as a military leader. When King Antiochus tried to have Hannibal instructed in military skills by an expert, the philosopher Phormios, Hannibal proved far ahead of such instruction. Legend has it that God had trained him better than any human expert could. That is why people eventually coined the saying: "The egg teaches the chicken, the sow is God's master, and Phormio equips Hannibal." Luther loved such humorous anecdotes and made them part of his own thought about secular power in the world. As he comments on Psalm 101:1 ("I will sing of loyalty and justice; to you, O Lord, will I sing"),

> The world is always full of such Phormios in all classes; they are called Master Smart Aleck, that infamous, dangerous man who can do everything better and still is not the man. And if a hundred others who had Hannibal's strength, courage, people, art, equipment, and everything, and still more, had been put in his place, they would not have been able to do what Hannibal did.[60]

Young David was Luther's biblical model of such a "wonderman" who defeated Goliath with a slingshot (1 Sam.17:49). In his own day, Luther perceived the Saxon duke, Frederick (called "the Wise"), to be such a "wonderman." Luther observed how others tried to imitate the duke, but they were foolish, not wise, because they only sought their own gain. Luther's satirical humor about such political fools shifts into high gear:

> It is as though a donkey wanted to play the harp and a sow wanted to spin because her paws are nimble and well qualified for it....But so things happen in the world: If God builds a church, the devil comes and builds a chapel beside it, yes, even countless chapels. And so here: If God raises up an outstanding man, either among the spiritual or the secular authorities, the devil brings his monkeys and simpletons to market to imitate everything. And yet it all amounts to monkey business and tomfoolery.[61]

In a more serious way, Luther told his congregation in sermons that there are two kinds of people: one kind tries hard to be successful but is not, even after years of trying; the other kind achieves everything they plan because the plans have been given divine timing. Such timing is an incredible and joyous experience; it is grounded in a faith that is no longer "anxious about tomorrow, for tomorrow will be anxious about itself" (Matt. 6:34).

> If God is kindly disposed to a man and gives him success, he can often accomplish more in one hour without care and anxiety than another man in four whole days with great care and anxiety. Whereas the one has dragged on with his anxiety and made it tedious for himself, the other has disposed of it in an hour. Thus no one can accomplish anything except when the hour comes that God gives as a free gift without our anxiety. It is vain for you to try to anticipate and with your concern to work out what you think are great schemes.[62]

Luther offers simple examples: the clock will not strike one before it has struck twelve; evening cannot come before the day is over; one must be a child before growing old; one cannot pick berries at Christmastime but one must wait until they are in season. Events have their appointed time, and human thought cannot produce them at will. But evil, the devil, always lies in wait as soon as one is baptized. Luther suggests a simple and direct way to oppose him: "Much less does he spare those of us who expose our backside to him [as a sign of mockery], who step before his very nose and preach as our duty demands about God's mercy and the devil's works."[63]

Luther also linked "the hour" of true opportunity with prayer. God needs to be consulted when something is planned to be done or is a reaction to certain experiences in life. Luther used the story of the arrest of Jesus in the Gospels as an example: Jesus was arrested when his hour had come, *not* because the enemies planned the event. But human minds are impatient and haughty, especially when assuming to carry out the will of God. Church leaders often act in this manner, and Luther suggests what God would say to them:

Our Lord God said: "My dear chief priests and bishops, not so fast! You had better consult Me, too, to find out whether the hour for this is at hand. Whenever you contemplate doing anything, it is well for you to ask Me whether My hour or My will is in your favor. If that hour has not come, all is useless." They say: "What is that hour to us? We will proceed with our plans nevertheless and fish ahead of the net." All right, go ahead—you will not catch any fish, but toads; for you have been interfering with the schedule.[64]

Accordingly, the mission of the church should be initiated by the quest for its divine permission. Luther tied Christian action in the world to the gift of divine timing, disclosed as an answer to prayer. One should act at specific times, chosen by God, and then give thanks for the opportunity to act on God's behalf. Such a spiritual stance creates true Christian freedom. "To become free implies that you fix your thoughts on something else than that which likes you.... You must direct your thoughts to something more exalted, namely, the Son of God who makes you free [John 8:36]."[65]

Luther linked his Christ-centered theology to daily life through the notion of the final "little hour," which determines every hour. In Christ, the second Adam, the final divine word about the fate of the world has been spoken. So Christian life on earth can return to its original intention embodied in the first Adam: to be in partnership with God as a stewardship of creation (to have "dominion" over other creatures, Gen. 1:26) according to human time penetrated by divine timing. God's original mandate to "dominate" was violated when Adam and Eve ate the forbidden fruit in order to "be like God" (Gen. 3:5). After their Fall they were called again by God to care for the world, but no longer according to their wishes but God's—at the appointed time. "Both prayer and God's commandment are more clearly understandable in the light of the concept of 'the time.'"[66] Prayer lets God direct all human actions and events, and the divine command is thereby heeded.

Luther's focus on the end time and its final "little hour" prevents any kind of theological speculation about divine "predestination" as *prediction*—that some are predestined to salvation and others to damnation; or chronological speculations about the end of the world. To Luther, any time used to do God's work already mirrors the final "little hour." God's power over all time is compressed into the hour when believers are called to do God's bidding; and then things truly change in a way no human mind can explain.

Luther was intrigued by the biblical saying in Eccles. 3:15, "That which is, already has been; that which is to be, already has been, and God seeks out what has gone by." It is another example of how steadfast is God in God's love and how selfish human creatures always want something new and different. Luther would object to the human speculation, popular in the saying that "the grass is always greener on the other side." He might agree, however, with the satirical twist of the proverb that "the grass is always greener over the septic tank." Luther learned that humans are dissatisfied with what is and always want what is to

be according to their liking. But God works
and acts in the opposite way.

> He does not turn away to future things.... God
> abides in the work that He does, and He does
> not overthrow it or run off to other and still
> other desires for the future, as the mind of
> man does. Those who walk according to God
> do this also; they are not diverted toward
> future things, to the neglect of the things that
> are present. The pious man does his work
> steadily and enjoys things steadily. *Because
> God seeks it even though it hinders Him.*[67]

When one stays on course to the final "little
hour," Luther contended, one will develop
an attitude of inner security and freedom,
no matter how crowded life becomes with
earthly problems. Reliance on the final "little
hour" as the transition to a new creation
creates an emotional space of inner peace
and joy already in the penultimate life of
sin, evil, and death.

Luther viewed vocation—the "walk of
life," the "station," or "office"—as the most
realistic means to use time in the light of the
Last Day. In this sense, "vocation" (*Beruf*)
is also a "calling" (*Berufung*) or summons
from God to obey his will. Vocations also
link people to each other in a relationship
of labor for the common good. God ordains
the time or the tasks of various vocations.
All vocations must be guided by the double

commandment of love, to love God and to love the neighbor as much as one loves oneself (Matt. 22:37–39). Luther was well aware how difficult it is to live like that. But he learned from the Bible that faith as anticipation of the Last Day and of a new creation overcomes tribulation and suffering in the various walks of earthly life.

> Here you see how faith is necessary in everything; how it makes all things easy, good and pleasant, even in prison or in death, as the martyrs prove. But without faith all things are difficult, bad and bitter, even if all the pleasures and jots of the whole world were yours, as is shown by all the mighty and the rich who live the most miserable life all the time.[68]

Luther felt born again when he experienced an inner emotional distance from his monastic life, which had been crowded with ever new ascetic rules for avoiding the divine punishment of inherited and accumulated sins. He was reborn free. His attitude was no longer shaped by terrible expectations (to appease an angry God) but by a joyful anticipation of the end of sin, death, and evil. The anticipation of the Last Day shaped Luther's life and thought in such a way that he felt free from "the terrors of heaven" that had driven him into the monastery.

Yielding to divine love, Luther shifted from an ascetic discipline of moral righteousness to a discipline of hope. Anticipating a future of never-ending life with God in Christ, Luther could endure the mean meantime between Christ's first and second advent with eschatological humor. In this way, Luther rediscovered and proclaimed the true foundation of the ancient Christian tradition: faith in the resurrection from the dead leading to faithful discipleship in this earthly life, empowered through Christ's presence in word and sacrament. That's enough to make one smile through the mean meantime!

Postscript

Luther asserted that faith in Christ alone creates freedom from sin, death, and evil. Christ reveals the unconditional love of God for human creatures who committed the worst and most senseless spiritual crime: to become gods themselves (Gen. 3:5). Luther likes to speak the language of the Gospel of John. Accordingly, Christ is the eternal Word, [which] became flesh and lived among us (John 1:1, 14). To Luther, the core of faith in Christ empowers believers to be perfectly free, subject to none; as the living Word of love, Christ is also the model for the believer to be a perfectly dutiful servant of all, subject to all.[1]

These two assertions mirrored for Luther the biblical double commandment of love: love of God and love of neighbor (Matt. 23:37–40). He viewed this double commandment as a guidepost on the highway of faith, characterized by its crossroad, the trek to eternal union with Christ and the threat of the abyss of evil, sin, and death. Luther summed up his stance by handing on the advice of Paul: to know nothing, except Jesus Christ, and him crucified (1 Cor. 2:2).[2] If a timid mind asks, Why? Luther responds: because the devil still prowls around like a roaring lion (1 Peter 5:9). But when you meet him, band together, stay cheerful, and laugh in his face. One should never argue with the devil, Luther counseled, but meet him with humor, ranging from a serene smile to scatological mocking. Humor is thus part of the essential spiritual food ration on the freedom march from the earthly to the heavenly city. Moreover, believers should never break ranks; they should stay together through thick and thin. Get away from yourself when evil tempts you, a contemporary Luther would admonish. Help someone in need. Use your mind to care for people in trouble; provide food and clothing for the poor; help the farmer spreading manure in the field; assist the victims of violence.

In our modern situation of organized social work, grounded in psychoanalysis, applying Luther's humor to the parable of the good Samaritan (Luke 10:25–37) could lead us to imagine the bad Samaritan saying to the victim: Whoever did this to you needs a lot of help. Too much analysis leads to paralysis.

Such psychological wisdom is illustrated by the use of one of Luther's witty proverbial expressions of scatological humor at one of the most conservative Roman Catholic places of pilgrimage in Austria: Mariazell, a center of Marian devotion. Vendors at the church offered a nicely framed saying, credited to Luther: Out of a desperate ass never comes a cheerful fart.[3]

Humor creates the freedom to laugh at one's own idiosyncrasies and not succumb to either a bitter-faced piety or useless theological calculations. One should let God be God, Luther insisted, and not wrest heaven from God.[4] Prayer outweighs pondering divine mysteries; and humorous musings about earthly riddles keep one's spiritual health better than various remedies of spiritual self-help. Humor is part of the power of the future promised to faithful disciples of Christ. Looking back, they can sing the ancient biblical song in the future tense: We will be like those who dream, and our mouth will be filled with laughter (Ps. 126:1-2).

Select Witticisms of Martin Luther

Holy Scripture does not deal much with great sinners like tax collectors and poor little whores because such people can also be recognized and judged by heathens. Rather, it deals with spiritual little worms and scorpions who pretend to have an appearance of holiness and great piety. (PK 15)

We have the tyrannical habit of animals when we eat. The wolf eats lambs, the fox eats chicken, geese—just as we do. Hawks and goshawks eat birds—just as we do. Pikes eat fish—just as we do. We also eat grass together with the oxen, horses and cows. We eat manure and dung together with the pigs; but everything becomes dung within us. (PK 35)

Whoever is never tempted knows nothing. (PK 36)

On the pulpit one should pull out the tits and feed simple folk with milk. For every day a new church grows up which must be very simply taught the doctrine for children. That is why one must diligently learn the catechism and thus distribute the milk. But the high, subtle and sharp thoughts and the strong wine one should reserve for "wiseacres" (*Klüglinge*). (PK 42)

Sadness is an instrument of the devil whereby he gets much accomplished. For the sadder and more preoccupied one is, the more successful the devil becomes....There fore, pray diligently and when you are sad, go to godly people and be consoled with the Word of God. (PK 52)

Thoughts are free; they, like desires, are not punished in a civic sense—but God is their judge. (PK 68)

The world is like a drunken peasant. If you lift him into the saddle on one side, he will fall off again on the other side. One can't help him, no matter how one tries. He wants to be the devil's. (TT 630, 1533. LW 54:111)

Where the lark is, the cuckoo also wants to be, for he thinks he could be a thousand times better than the lark. The pope does exactly the same, puts himself into the church and is louder than anyone else—so, come what may, one must hear his song. But just as the cuckoo has his use—he indicates that summer is near—so does the pope: he serves to proclaim that the Last Day is not far away. (PK 89)

Whoever is not handsome at twenty, not strong at thirty, not wise at forty and is not rich at fifty might as well give up hope. Age does not protect against foolishness. (PK 103)

When Christ has the trumpet blown at the Last Day, everyone will pop up and be resurrected like flies who lie dead in the winter. (PK 110)

Surely, there will be dogs and other animals in the kingdom of heaven because the earth will not be empty and desolate....God will create a new heaven and a new earth, and also new little dogs. Their skin will be like gold and their hair like jewelry. Animals will not devour each other like frogs, snakes and other poisonous animals who are poisonous and dangerous because of original sin. These animals will then not only be not harmful to us, but they will be delightful, joyous and pleasant so that we can even play with them. (PK 114)

He [an opponent] is an excellent man, as skillful, clever and versed in Holy Scripture as a cow in a walnut tree, or a sow on a harp. (Against Hanswurst [1541]. WA 51, 522:21–22. LW 41:219)

Justice is always an honest man, but the judge is often a rogue. (WA 51, 554:19–20. LW 41:245)

The Franciscans are the lice which the devil put into the fur-coat of God. (TT No. 301, 1532. WATR 1, 125:1–2)

The bishops didn't dare touch a single monk because when a sow cries out the whole herd comes running. (TR No. 416, 1542/43. TR 5, 222:17–18. LW 54:68)

If our Lord God can pardon me for having crucified and martyred him for about twenty years [by saying mass], he can also approve of my occasional taking a drink in his honor. God grant it, no matter how the world may wish to interpret it! (TT No. 139, 1531. WATR 1, 60. LW 54:20)

Tomorrow I have to lecture on the drunkenness of Noah [Gen. 9:20–27], so I should drink enough this evening to be able to talk about that wickedness as one who knows by experience. (TT No. 3476. LW 54:207)

The Epistle to the Galatians is my dear epistle. I have put my confidence in it. It is my Katie von Bora [Luther's wife]. (TT No. 146, 1532. LW 54:20)

A load of hay must give way to a drunken man. (WA 50, 566:5–7. LW 41:76)

No one can win his spurs against sick people. (Ibid.)

No one can become an expert among ignoramuses. (Ibid.)

Many a man speaks ill of women without knowing what his mother did. (TH 36:11)

Many hands make labor easy. (TH 50:22)

The game of the cats is the death of the mice. (TH 62:35)

An old debt does not rust. (TH 85:63)

Some people need a fig-leaf on their mouths. (TH 105:86)

Quiet waters are deep. (TH 122:105)

The bird sings according to the size of its beak. (TH 133:121)

Whoever wants to be with wolves has to howl with them. (TH 370:409)

The church is a mouth-house rather than a pen-house. (WA 10 1/2, 48:5)

Let Christians drill themselves in the catechism....Let them never stop until they have taught the devil to death and have become more learned than God himself and all his saints. (BC 383:19)

[When Luther could not attend the wedding of his friend George Spalatin, he wrote a letter with an erotic passage, the second part of which was stricken from early editions of Luther's correspondence:] When you sleep with your Catherine and embrace her, you should think, 'This child of man, this wonderful creature of God has been given to me by my Christ. May he be praised and glorified.' On the evening of the day on which, according to my calculations, you will receive this, I shall make love to my Catherine while you make love to yours, and thus we will be united in love. (Letter of December 6, 1525. WABr 3, 635:22–28)

Abbreviations

BC   *The Book of Concord. The Confessions of the Evangelical Lutheran Church.* Edited by Robert Kolb and Timothy J. Wengert. Minneapolis: Fortress Press, 2000.

BS   *Die Bekenntnisschriften der evangelisch-lutherischen Kirche.* 3d ed. Göttingen: Vandenhoeck & Ruprecht, 1930.

LW   *Luther's Works.* American ed. 55 vols. Edited by Jaroslav Pelikan and Helmut Lehmann. Philadelphia: Fortress Press; St. Louis: Concordia, 1955–1986.

PK   Peter Karner (ed.). *Die Welt is wie ein betrunkener Bauer. Aus den Tischreden Martin Luthers.* 4th ed. Vienna, Freiburg, Basel: Herder, 1983.

TH   Thiele, Ernst (ed.). *Luthers Sprichwörtersammlung.* Weimar: Böhlaus Nachfolger, 1900.

WA   *Luthers Werke: Kritische Gesamtausgabe. Schriften.* 65 vols. Weimar: H. Böhlau, 1883–1993.

WABr   *Luthers Werke: Kritische Gesamtausgabe. Briefwechsel.* 18 vols. Weimar: H. Böhlau, 1930–1985.

WATR   *Luthers Werke: Kritische Gesamtausgabe. Tischreden.* 6 vols. Weimar: H. Böhlau, 1912–1921.

Notes

Preface

1. *Humor och Melankoli och andra Lutherstudier* (Uppsala: Published by the Swedish Student Movement, 1919). German summary by Peter Katz, "Humor und Melancholie und andere Lutherstudien von Nathan Söderblom," *Luther* 5 (1923), 63-65. All translations mine.

2. Söderblom did a peculiar study on the relationship between Luther's trust in God and mysticism. See "Die Ausmündung der Mystik in Luthers Gottvertrauen" in Katz, 64. The title also reflects Söderblom's basic stance—God is revealed in all religions—defended in his major work, *The Living God* (Edinburgh: T. & T. Clark, 1933).

3. Fritz Blanke, *Luthers Humor: Scherz und Schalk in Luthers Seelsorge* (Hamburg: Furche Verlag, 1957).

4. *Martin—God's Court Jester. Luther in Retrospect*, 2d ed. (Ramsey, N.J.: Sigler, 1991), 197-202. "Luther's Humor: Instrument of Witness," *Dialog* 22 (1983): 176-81. "Der Humor bei Martin Luther," *Lutherjahrbuch* 63 (1996): 19-38. "Luther on Humor," *Lutheran Quarterly* 18 (2004): 373-86.

5. This was the aim of bygone Roman Catholic polemics, exemplified by Heinrich Denifle (1844-1905). See also Heiko A. Oberman, *Luther: Man Between God and the Devil*, tr. Eileen Walliser-Schwarzbart (New Haven: Yale University Press, 1989), 278.

Introduction

1. For example, *Webster's New Collegiate Dictionary* (Springfield, Mass.: Merriam, 1975).

2. Kuno Fischer, *Über den Witz. Ein philosophischer Essay* (Tübingen: Klöpfer and Meyer, 1996), 113.

3. So defined by the modern humorist Dave Barry. See Bryan Curtis, "Dave Barry," The Middlebrow, *Slate* (January 14, 2005).

4. Jan Bremmer and Herman Roodenburg (eds.), *Kulturgeschichte des Humors. Von der Antike bis heute* (tr. Kai Brodersen, Darmstadt: Wissenschaftliche

Buchgesellschaft, 1999), 9. I had access only to the German translation of the book.

5. Table Talk No. 352, 1532. WATR 1, 146:12-14. LW 54:50. Sermons on the Gospel of John (3:14), 1539. WA 47, 66:21-24. LW 22:339.

6. WA 7, 38:6-12. LW 31:371. Emphasis mine to indicate the vision of faith of Christ's second coming.

7. Computation of the Ages of the World (*Supputatio annorum mundi*), 1541. WA. 53, 10-15. Details in Eric W. Gritsch, *Martin—God's Court Jester. Luther in Retrospect*, 2d ed. (Ramsey, N.J.: Sigler, 1991), 100.

8. Table Talk No. 5537, 1542-1543. WATR 5, 222:17-20. LW 54:448.

9. Table Talk No. 5010, 1540. WATR 4, 611:11-16. LW 54:377.

10. Sermon on Matt. 27:33-36 in *Hauspostille* (Home-Postil), 1545. WA 52, 800:1-6. I am grateful to Pastor Georg Heckel for providing this text. See also Helmut Thielicke, *Das Lachen der Heiligen und Narren: Nachdenkl. über Witz und Humor.* (Freiburg: Herder, 1988), 96: "The message, which is embedded in humor and nourishes it, is the proclamation (*Kerygma*) that the world is overcome." This view is also shared by Kurt Hübner, "Meditation über Humor und Christentum," *Zeitschrift für Theologie und Kirche* 96 (1999): 508-24.

The Power of Serenity

1. Table Talk No. 122, 1531. WATR1, 48:10-11. LW 54:16.

2. Letter of November 21, 1521. WABr 8, 573:30-574:2. LW 48:332.

3. Table Talk No. 94, 1531. WA 1, 35:17-20. LW 54:11.

4. "Table Talks" Nos. 2255a, 1531. 4091, 1540. 5371, 1541. WATR 2, 379:7-19. 4, 129:30-130:2. 5, 98:21-28.

5. "Infiltrating and Clandestine Preachers" (1532), WA 30:3, 522:2-3. LW 40:387-388.

6. Letter of May 30, 1518. LW 48:66. Italics mine.

7. Letter to John Lang, October 26, 1518. WABr 1, 525:11-13. LW 48:27-28

8. Table Talk No. 3232c, 1532. WATR 3, 228:31-32. LW 54:194. The variant 3232b calls the place of the

experience "the lavatory" (*cloaca*). WATR 3, 228:23. Details in LW 54:193, n. 64.

9. "Preface to the Complete Edition of Latin Writings" (1545). WA 54, 185:21–186:2. LW 34:336–7.

10. WA 54, 186:8–14. Italics mine.

11. Lectures on Galatians (1535). WA/1, 589:25–28. LW 26:387. Italics mine.

12. WA 1, 234, 4:33–34. LW 31:28. The legend claimed that the two saints, Pope Severinus (638–640) and Pope Paschal I (817–824), preferred to remain longer in purgatory so that they might have greater glory in heaven.

13. See the brief sketch on "continuity and change" regarding the history of fools, rogues, and court jesters in Bremmer and Roodenburg, *Kulturgeschichte des Humors*, 104–8.

14. "On the Papacy in Rome" (1520). WA 6, 286:20–26. LW 39:57. Italics mine.

15. WA 6, 323:35–324:4. LW 39:104.

16. Luther's designation of the hiding place. Patmos was the island where John, the writer of the Apocalypse, was exiled (Rev. 1:9). See his letters of May 26 and June 1, 1521. WABr 6, 349:101. 140:6. LW 48:236, 247.

17. Letter of December 1, 1521. WABr 2, 407:66–72. LW 48:341–2.

18. WABr 2, 421:15–16.

19. "Against the Spiritual Estate of the Pope and the Bishops, Falsely So Called" (1522). WA 10/2, 105–158. LW 39:247–99.

20. Martin Brecht, *Martin Luther*, tr. James L. Schaaf, 3 vols. (Minneapolis: Fortress, 1985–1993), 2:201.

21. Details in Brecht, *Martin Luther*, 2:42–3.

22. "To the Christian Nobility of the German Nation," (1520). WA 6, 404:232–405:3. LW 44:123–4. Italics mine.

23. WA 6, 448:26. LW 44:187.

24. "A Sincere Admonition to All Christians" (1522). WA 8, 685:5–11. LW 45:70–1.

25. "On Temporal Authority" (1523). WA 11, 247:3–11. LW 45:84.

26. WA 11, 267:30–31. LW 45:113.

27. "To the Councilmen of All Cities in Germany" (1524).

WA 15, 27:15–16. LW 45:347.

28. A proverbial expression. WA 15, 33:9–13. LW 45: 353–54.

29. Letter to Justus Jonas, April 24, 1530. WABr 5, 289:12–16.

30. Letter to Spalatin, April 24, 1530. WABr 5, 291:46–47. LW 49:293.

31. WABr 5, 291:39–42. LW 49:294–295.

32. WA 30/3, 291:9–13. LW 47:29–30.

33. Lectures on Gal. 2:6, 1535. WA 40/1, 181:11–13. LW 26:99.

34. Published by the Lutheran World Federation and the Pontifical Council for Promoting Christian Unity (Geneva, 1995).

35. The visit of Vergerio, recorded in various sources, is summarized in Brecht, *Martin Luther*, 3:174–6.

36. WA 53, 404–5.

37. See, for example, his letter of May 18, 1518, addressed to George Spalatin. WABr 1, 174. LW 48:63.

38. Roland H. Bainton, *Here I Stand* (Nashville: Abingdon-Cokesbury, 1950), 298.

39. WA 7, 262–283, 621–688. WA 8, 247–254. LW 39:111–238.

40. WA 7, 262:1–16. LW 39:111, 112.

41. WA 7, 228:1–4. LW 39:151.

42. WA 7, 645:18–23. LW 39:172.

43. WA 8, 251:14–17. LW 39:234.

44. "Against the Spiritual Estate of the Pope" (1522). WA 10/1–2, 105:1–2. LW 39:247.

45. WA 10/2, 106:10–14. LW 39:248. Luther's reference to his "bestial character" was a reference to the bull *Exsurge, Domine*, which called Luther a "wild boar."

46. "Doctor Martin Luther's Bull and Reformation" (1522). New editions in 1523. WA 10/2, 140–58. LW 39:278–99.

47. "On the Councils and the Church" (1539). WA 50, 611:6–18. LW 41:127–8.

48. WA 50, 644:12–13. LW 41:167.

49. Against Hanswurst, 1541. WA 51, 533:18–35. LW 41:244–5.

50. "Against the Roman Papacy, an Institution of the Devil" (1545). WA 54, 206–99. LW 41:263–376.

51. Many of the illustrations can be found in Brecht, *Martin Luther*, vol. 3, ch. 13, sec. 3.

52. "Against the Roman Papacy, an Institution of the Devil" (1545). WA 54, 206:1. LW 41:263.

53. WA 54, 215:8. LW 41:273.

54. WA 54, 220:35–221:8. 299:6–9. LW 41:280, 376.

55. "Confession Concerning Christ's Supper" (1528). WA 26, 348:32–33. LW 37:235.

56. WA 26, 471:23. LW 37:329.

57. "The Bondage of the Will" (1525). WA 18, 600:13–601:11. LW 33:15–16.

58. WA 18, 787:1–3. LW 33:295.

Wit and Witness

1. This section uses materials from my essay "Luther's Humor as a Tool for Interpreting Scripture" in *Biblical Hermeneutics in Historical Perspective: Studies in Honor of Karlfried Froehlich on His Sixtieth Birthday*, ed. Mark S. Burrows and Paul Rorem (Grand Rapids: Eerdmans, 1991), 187–97.

2. Commentary on Ps. 2:4, 1532. WA 40/2, 219:31–32. LW 12:23.

3. WA 40/2, 226:14–22. LW 12:28. It is an accident of history and its irony that one of Luther's modern detractors agrees with this dialectic of faith and humor—Reinhold Niebuhr (1892–1971). He had accused Luther of making a disastrous distinction between a "private" and an "official ethic," thus encouraging tyranny in Germany during the regime of Adolf Hilter (1933–1945). See *The Nature and Destiny of Man*, 2 vols. (New York: Scribner's Sons, 1953), 2:194–5. But Niebuhr sounded like Luther when he declared in a sermon: "Humor is concerned with the immediate incongruities of life and faith with the ultimate ones.... Laughter is our reaction to immediate incongruities and those which do not affect us essentially. Faith is the only possible response to the ultimate incongruities of existence which threaten the very meaning of life.... Humor is, in fact, a prelude to faith; and laughter is the beginning

of prayer. Laughter must be heard in the outer courts of religion; and the echoes of it should resound in the sanctuary; but there is no laughter in the holy of holies. There laughter is swallowed up in prayer and humor is fulfilled by faith." See *Humor and Faith. Discerning the Signs of the Times: Sermons for Today and Tomorrow* (New York: Scribner's Sons, 1946), 111–12.

4. Lectures on Genesis, 1535–1545. WA 42–44. LW 1–8. I am using the 1535 series of lectures.

5. Table Talk No. 146, 1532. WATR 1, 69:18–20. LW 54:20.

6. *Webster's New Collegiate Dictionary.*

7. WA 42, 22:4–10. LW 1:28. Emphasis mine.

8. WA 42, 39:1–14. LW 1:52. Emphasis mine.

9. WA 42, 40:43–44. LW 1:62.

10. WA 42, 62:7–10. LW 1:82.

11. WA 42, 80:12–14. LW 1:105.

12. WA 42, 251:39–40. LW 1:342.

13. WA 42, 309:36–39.. LW 2:67,69.

14. WA 42, 365:11–13.. LW 2:147.

15. WA 42, 365:18–21. LW 2:147.

16. WA 42, 368:23–27. LW 2:152.

17. WA 42, 505:15–18. LW 2:340.

18. WA 42, 552:11–14. LW 3:5.

19. WA 43, 55:27–29. LW 3:252.

20. WA 43, 67:15–21. LW 3:268.

21. WA 43, 73:14–19. LW 3:277.

22. WA 43, 195:35–36. LW 3:308.

23. WA 43, 97:14–19. LW 3:310.

24. WA 43, 98:10–16. LW 3:310, 311.

25. WA 43, 98:25–28. LW 3:312.

26. WA 43, 216:20–23. LW 4:113.

27. WA 43, 217:34–35, 37–38. LW 4:189.

28. WA 43, 349:19–21. LW 4:297.

29. WA 43, 354:36–40. LW 4:304–5.

30. WA 43, 454:3–5. LW 5:37.

31. WA 44, 43:26. LW 6:59.

32. WA 44, 99:27–32. LW 6:133.

33. WA 40/1, 204:17–18. LW 26:113.

34. WA 40/1, 207:28–208:13. LW 26:116.

35. WA 40/1, 241:14-16. LW 26:137-8.

36. WA 40/1, 206:34-207:25. LW 26:156.

37. WA 40/1, 276:28-32. LW 26:162.

38. WA 40/1, 523:6-9. LW 26:340.

39. Quoted from Roland H. Bainton, *The Martin Luther Christmas Book* (Philadelphia: Fortress, 1958), 38. Original texts selected from sermons in WA 22.

40. Letter of June 1540 to Elector John Frederick. WABr 9, 134:45-7.

41. Ibid., 134:68-70.

42. Table Talk No. 5063. WATR 4, 640:1-6.

43. Letter dated December 4, 1539. WABr 8, 622:29-623:37.

44. Ibid., 625:11-626:36.

45. Ibid., 626:48-49.

46. 1534? WA 38, 292-293.

47. Letter of July 9, 1535. WABr 7, 307:11-14.

48. "Whether One May Flee From a Deadly Plague" (1527). WA 23, 356:11-14, 29-32, 358:3-4, 10-11. LW 43:128.

49. For example, see a letter dated October 4, 1529. WABr 5, 154. LW 49:236.

50. Letter of February 10, 1546. WABr 8, 626:48-49. LW 50:305-6.

51. *Webster's New Collegiate Dictionary.*

52. Table Talk No. 4465, 1539. WATR 4, 325:22-24. LW 54:343. Italics mine.

53. 1545. WA 54, 188-194. LW 34:363-6.

54. Table Talk No. 3595, 1537. WATR 3, 440-441. LW 54:238.

55. Lectures on Genesis, 1545. WA 44, 718:36-719:6. LW 8:191. Italics mine.

56. Lectures on Genesis, 1541-1542. WA 43, 533:9-20. LW 5:152.

57. Lectures on Genesis, 1542-1544. WA 44, 42:38-43:5. LW 6:58.

58. WA 44, 300:9-16. 25-26. 29-30. LW 6: 401.

59. Notes on Ecclesiastes, 1530. WA 20, 161:34-162:3. LW 15, 149. Emphasis mine.

60. Letter to John Rühel, brother-in-law, dated May 4, 1525. WABr 3, 481:64-482:3. LW 49:111.

61. Letter of October 4, 1530. WABr 5, 639:30–35. LW 49:428–429.

62. Letter of July 9, 1545. WABr 11, 132:26–29. LW 50:267.

63. Letter of December 6, 1545. WA, Br 11, 226. LW 50:284.

64. Letter to Elector John Frederick, dated March 28, 1532. WABr 6, 277:19.

65. Table Talk No. 122, 1531. WATR 1, 48:9–13, 17–21. LW 54:16. One of the most popular eschatological sayings of Luther cannot be found in his writings: "If I knew that the world would end tomorrow I would still plant a little apple tree today." The saying appeared in Germany after World War II and was attributed to Luther—it sounded just like him! See Martin Schloemann, *Luthers Apfelbäumchen. Bemerkungen zu Optimismus und Pessimismus im christlichen Selbstverständnis* (Wuppertaler Hoschschulreden 7, Wuppertal: Peter Hammer Verlag, 1975).

66. "Preface to the Wittenberg Edition of Luther's German Writings" (1539). WA 50, 658:1–4, 660:31–661:5. LW 34:284, 287–288.

Smiling through the Mean Meantime

1. Table Talk No. 4018, 1538. WATR 4, 78:29–79:2. LW 54:310.

2. "Lectures on Galatians" (1535). WA 40, 596:21–27. LW 26, 391–392.

3. *The Bondage of the Will* (1525). WA 18, 685:27–686:3. LW 33:140.

4. Table Talk No. 5070, 1540. WATR 4, 641:14–18.20–642:2. LW 54:385.

5. Table Talk No. 153, 1532. WATR 1, 72:17–18. LW 54:22.

6. Table Talk No. 5534, 1542–1543. WATR 5, 219:29–220:4. LW 54:448.

7. "Commentary on Psalm 51" (1532). WA 40/2, 328:17–24. LW 12:311.

8. "Lectures on Romans" (1515–1516). WA 56, 37:27. LW 25:361.

9. *Smalcald Articles* (1537). II, 1, 4, 5. BS 415. BC 301.

10. *Rhapsodia* (1530). WA 30/2, 357–376.

11. *Nun freut euch liebe Christen gemein* (1532). WA 35, 422–425; three melodies, ibid., 493–495. LW 53:219-220. Modern title, "Dear Christians, one and All, Rejoice," *Lutheran Book of Worship* (Minneapolis: Augsburg, 1978), no. 299.

12. Martin Luther to the Devotees of Music: Preface to George Rhau's *Delightful Symphonies* (1538). WA 50, 371:1-13. LW 53:323.

13. Letter of July 16, 1540. WABr 9, 174–175. LW 50:218-20.

14. Table Talk No. 3476, 1536. WATR 3, 344:22-25. LW 54:207. The last line is as close as Luther ever got to the couplet once attributed to him: "He who loves not women, wine and song, remains a fool his whole life long."

15. "Lectures on Galatians" (1535). WA 40/1, 284:4-7, 286:15-17. LW 26:168.

16. The Freedom of the Christian, 1520. WA 7, 55:3-4. LW 31:351.

17. WA 7, 55:7. LW 31:351. More expressive in German: "a cheerful exchange" (ein fröhlicher Wechsel). WA 7, 25:34.

18. WA 7, 55:7-20. LW 31: 352.

19. "Third Disputation Against the Antinomians" (1538). WA 39/1, 521:5-522:3, cited in Gerhard Ebeling, *Luther: An Introduction to His Thought*, tr. R. A. Wilson (Philadelphia: Fortress, 1970), 163-164.

20. Table Talk No. 3339, 1533. WATR 3, 276:26-27.

21. Sermon on Matt. 25:31-46 (Nov. 27, 1537). WA 45, 329:20-22.

22. *Large Catechism* (1529). Explanation of the Third Article of the Creed. BS 659:57. BC 238:57.

23. *Small Catechism* (1529). On Baptism. BS 516:12. BC 360:12.

24. *Large Catechism* (1529). The Lord's Supper. BS 712:24. BC 469:24.

25. "The Three Symbols or Creeds of the Church" (1538). WA 50, 272:32-273:1. LW 34:215.

26. "Lectures on Genesis" (1535/36). WA 42, 376. LW 2:163.

27. Lectures on Genesis 2:3, "God blessed the seventh day" (1535). WA 42, 61:4–5, 9–11, 15–19. LW 1:80, 81.
28. Table Talk No. 274, 1532. WATR 1, 115:31–116:1. LW 54:38.
29. *Large Catechism* (1529). Third Article of the Creed, 58. BS 659. BC 438.
30. Letter to John Rühel, a lawyer friend, May 4, 1525. WABr 3, 482:1–3. LW 49:111.
31. Table Talk No. 3178a, 1532. WATR 3, 211:15–21. LW 54:191.
32. Table Talk No. 4364, 15639. WATR 4, 262:15–19. LW 54:334.
33. Table Talk No. 1631, 1532. WATR 2, 156:25–30. LW 54:159.
34. Table Talk No. 5498, 1542. WATR 5, 193:12–15. LW 54:432.
35. Letter to Philip Melanchthon, dated July 29, 1539. WABr 5, 406:34–42. LW 49:329–330.
36. Table Talk No. 3006a, 1533. WATR 5, 138:33–35. LW 54:189.
37. Table Talk No. 3543A, 1537. WATR 3, 390:15–18. LW 54:227.
38. Table Talk No. 3553, 1537. WATR 3, 404:8–13. LW 54:232.
39. Letter to Wenceslas Link, dated June 20, 1543. WABr 10, 335:12–13. LW 50:242.
40. Letter of February 1, 1546. WABr 11, 276:13–15, 19–22. LW 50:291.
41. Sermon in November 1528. WA 27, 409:19–411:4.
42. WA 29, 401:29–36.
43. WA 29, 83:20–25. WA 32, 4:10–15.
44. Sermon on July 16, 1531. WA 34/2, 8:15–27.
45. "Infiltrating and Clandestine Preachers" (1532). WA 30/3, 518–527. LW 40:383–94.
46. "The Sermon on the Mount" (1538). WA 32, 495:15–496:2. LW 21:237.
47. Table Talk No. 2803. WATR 3, 13:6.
48. Table Talk No. 2803. WATR 3, 1:15–16.
49. Letter to Justus Jonas, dated October 28, 1535. WABr 7, 317:15–17. LW 50:108.
50. Table Talk No. 1154a. WATR 1, 571:6–9.

51. Letter of August 29, 1535. WABr 7, 215:16–18. LW 50:87.

52. Letter to the bishop of Bremen, dated March 26, 1542. WABr 10, 23:4–5.

53. Table Talks Nos. 3818, 6238, 4309, WATR 3, 637. 4, 206–210. 5, 554.

54. Table Talk No. 4542, 1539. WATR 4, 369:6–7, 9–11. LW 54:351.

55. Recorded as Table Talk No. 5677, 1546. WATR 5, 318:3. LW 54:476.

56. This is well summarized in the context of vocation in the classic study of Gustaf Wingren, *Luther on Vocation*, Tr. Carl C. Rasmussen (Evansville, Ind.: Ballast, 1999). Reprint of the English ed. of 1959. Original Swedish ed. 1949.

57. Wingren, 213.

58. "Notes on Ecclesiastes" (1526). WA 30, 58:26–28, 33–34. 59:14–16. LW 15:49:50.

59. Wingren, 214.

60. Commentary on Psalm 101, 134. WA 51, 208:28–33. LW 13:156.

61. WA 11, 211:2–4, 6–13. LW 13:159.

62. "Sermons on the Sermon on the Mount" (1536). WA 32, 471:5–12. LW 21:207–8.

63. Sermons on John 7:30 ("his [Jesus'] hour has not yet come"), 1532. WA 33, 408:11–16. LW 23:257.

64. WA 33, 405:10–406:9. LW 23:255.

65. WA 33, 665:11–14. LW 23:410.

66. Wingren, 220.

67. Notes on Ecclesiastes, 1526. WA 20, 66:22–27. LW 15:56.

68. "Sermons (*Kirchenpostille*)" (1522). WA 10/1, 316:9–14.

Postscript

1. "The Freedom of the Christian" (1520). WA 7, 21:1-4. LW 31:344.

2. Lectures on Romans, 1534. WA 37, 661:20-26. LW 25:361.

3. PK, 8.

4. *The Large Catechism* (1529). The First Commandment 22. BS 565. BC 388.

Bibliography

Bainton, Roland, H. *Here I Stand*. Nashville: Abingdon-Cokesbury, 1950.

Blanke, Fritz, *Luthers Humor: Scherz und Schalk in Luthers Seelsorge*. Hamburg: Furche, 1967.

Brecht, Martin. *Martin Luther*. 3 vols. Trans. James L. Schaaf. Minneapolis: Fortress Press, 1965–1993.

Bremmer, Jan and Herman Roodenburg, eds. *Kulturgeschichte des Humors: Von der Antike bis heute*. Trans. Kai Brodersen. Darmstadt: Wissenschaftliche Buchgesellschaft, 1999.

Ebeling, Gerhard. *Luther: An Introduction to His Thought*. Trans. R. A. Wilson. Philadelphia: Fortress Press, 1970.

Fischer, Kuno. *Über den Witz: Ein philosophischer Essay*. Tübingen: Klöpfer und Meyer, 1996.

Gritsch, Eric W. "Luther's Humor: Instrument of Witness," *Dialog* 22 (1983):176–81.

_____. *Martin—God's Court Jester: Luther in Retrospect*. 2d ed. Ramsey, N.J.: Sigler, 1990.

_____. "Luther's Humor as a Tool for Interpreting Scripture," in Mark S. Burrows and Paul Rorem, eds. *Biblical Hermeneutics in Historical Perspective: Studies in Honor of Karlfried Froehlich on His Sixtieth Birthday*. Grand Rapids: Eerdmans, 1991:187–97.

_____. "Der Humor bei Martin Luther," *Lutherjahrbuch* 63 (1996):19–38.

_____. "Luther on Humor," *Lutheran Quarterly* 28 (2004):373–86.

Hübner, Karl. "Meditation über Humor und Christentum," *Zeitschrift für Theologie und Kirche* 96 (1999):508–24.

Lutheran Book of Worship. Minneapolis: Augsburg, 1978.

Niebuhr, Reinhold. *Humor and Faith: Discerning the Signs of the Times: Sermons for Today and Tomorrow*. New York: Scribner's Sons, 1946.

_____. *The Nature and Destiny of Man*. 2 vols. New York: Scribner's Sons, 1953.

Schloemann, Martin. *Luthers Apfelbäumchen: Bemerkungen zu Optimismus und Pessimismus im christlichen Selbstverständnis*. Wuppertaler Hochschulreden 7. Wuppertal: Peter Hammer, 1975.

Söderblom, Nathan. *Humor och Melankoli och andre Lutherstudier*. Uppsala: Swedish Student Movement, 1919. German summary in Peter Katz, "Humor und Melancholie und andere Lutherstudien von Nathan Söderblom," *Luther* 5 (1923):63–65

Thielicke, Helmut. *Das Lachen der Heiligen und Narren: Nachdenkl. über Witz und Humor*. Freiburg: Herder, 1988.

Webster's New Collegiate Dictionary. Springfield, Mass.: Merriam, 1975.

Wingren, Gustaf. *Luther on Vocation*. Trans. Carl C. Rasmussen. Evansville, Ind.: Ballast, 1999. Original Swedish ed., 1942.